Trade Finance Handbook

Alan J. Beard
Richard M. Thomas

Australia · Brazil · Canada · Mexico · Singapore · Spain · United Kingdom · United States

Trade Finance Handbook

Alan J. Beard, Richard M. Thomas

COPYRIGHT © 2006 by Texere, an imprint of Thomson/South-Western, a part of The Thomson Corporation. Thomson and the Star logo are trademarks used herein under license.

Composed by: Interactive Composition Corporation

Printed in the United States of America by RR Donnelley, Crawfordsville

1 2 3 4 5 08 07 06 05
This book is printed on acid-free paper.

ISBN 0-324-30521-4

Library of Congress Cataloging in Publication Number is available. See page 216 for details.

For more information about our products, contact us at:

Thomson Learning
Academic Resource
Center 1-800-423-0563

Thomson Higher Education
5191 Natorp Boulevard
Mason, Ohio 45040
USA

CONTENTS

ACKNOWLEDGMENTS

A book like this requires the commitment of many participants. The authors express their deepest gratitude to Eric Green for his tireless efforts as the project manager. His contributions were incalculable. We are also grateful to Sabrina Nguyen for her extraordinary work refining the final manuscript.

The term finance section of this book was greatly enhanced by Michael R. Czinkota, who provided generous input and advice. Carey D. Fiertz was a great asset in preparing the case studies and providing background information. Special thanks go to the staff at Interlink Capital Strategies, Jozsef Szamosfalvi, Juan Fronjosa, Jim Tomkins, Lew Cramer, Brady E. Edholm, and Donald Burley for providing additional materials and suggestions. They all encouraged and supported us. If this book assists in the realization of export transaction that helps spur economic development, then we consider our efforts a success.

Alan J. Beard
Richard M. Thomas

ABOUT THE AUTHORS

Alan J. Beard is the Managing Director of Interlink Capital Strategies, a Washington DC-based consulting firm specializing in emerging market finance and international business development. Previously Mr. Beard joined and successfully grew a similar consulting firm that was acquired by JP Morgan Chase (formerly Bank One). During his employment, that firm arranged over $9 billion in government grants, equity, guarantees, and loans for more than 700 companies. Mr. Beard also established and headed up the international merchant banking unit of Bank One Capital Corp. and worked in the Latin America and U.S. divisions of the Export-Import Bank and the Department of Commerce's International Trade Administration. He has been a frequent speaker, university lecturer, and published writer on international business and finance issues. Currently, he is an adjunct professor at Georgetown University McDonough School of Business. He has edited, co-authored, and contributed to the writing of more than 25 books, including *Terrorism & Personal Security, Inside the World's Export Credit Agencies,* and *Inside the World's Development Finance Institutions,* recently published by Thomson Publishing. Mr. Beard graduated from the University of Utah cum laude and received his MBA from the George Washington University. He has lived and worked extensively in Latin America and Europe.

Richard M. "Chip" Thomas completed his BA from Southern Illinois University in 1969, majoring in economics and history, and completed a master's degree in 1975 from the American Graduate School of International Management. Mr. Thomas has a 20-year career in international banking, specializing in international trade and finance. During his banking career, Mr. Thomas developed a skill in training and was responsible for International Product and Service Training for Mellon Bank's customers and employees. In 1995, he left banking to pursue his interest in training by helping to establish the American Export Training Institute (AETI), which provides practical training in export finance to corporations and financial institutions throughout the United States and Canada.

ABOUT INTERLINK PUBLICATIONS

Interlink Publications is part of Interlink Capital Strategies (www. i-caps. com), a 10-year-old Washington DC-based consulting firm specializing in emerging market finance and business development. Our managers are experts in international project financing, trade financing, raising private equity, business development, and marketing with a Washington insider's expertise on how to access government programs and political support for international business transactions. They have successfully arranged billions of dollars of financing and used government advocacy and strategic industry relations to structure transactions worldwide. Clients include National City Bank, JP Morgan Chase, Sovereign Bank, Zions Bank, Corning, L-3 Communications, CP Group (Thailand), Clark Construction, and Orbital Science Corporation, as well as many small and medium sized enterprises. Interlink Publications has been successful in creating a number of handbooks useful to international business executives, including most recently *Finding the Priority Pathway: Overcoming Organizational Obstacles* and *Terrorism & Personal Security*.

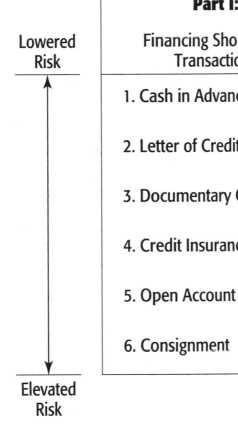

Lowered
Risk

Elevated
Risk

Part I:

Financing Short-Term
Transactions

1. Cash in Advance

2. Letter of Credit

3. Documentary Collections

4. Credit Insurance

5. Open Account

6. Consignment

INTRODUCTION

A. Why a Book on International Trade Finance?

Since 1960, there has been an explosive growth in the export of U.S. goods and services.

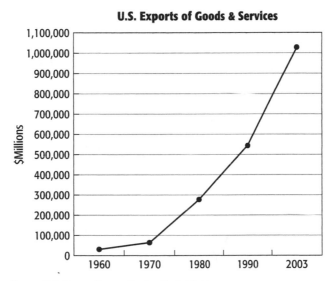

U.S. Exports of Goods & Services

Source: U.S. Census Bureau, Foreign Trade Division.

In each of the last three decades, the volume of exports was at least double the volume of the previous decade. Large U.S. companies accounted for 71 percent of total value of U.S. exports, but small to medium size enterprises (SMEs) accounted for 97 percent of total export volume. In fact, by any significant measure, SMEs are the dominant force in U.S. exports. Consider the following statistics from the International Trade Administration:[1]

- The number of SME exporters grew 99.7 percent between 1992 and 2002, a figure that was over double the growth of large company exporters.

---

[1] *Small and Medium-Sized Exporting Companies: A Statistical Handbook.* U.S. Department of Commerce, International Trade Administration. June 2005.

- In all major product categories, SME exporters outnumber large firms. For example, SMEs comprise 94 percent of all exporters of machinery manufactures, 93 percent of computers and electronic products, and 92 percent of transportation equipment.
- More than two-thirds of U.S. exporters have fewer than 20 employees.
- More than two-thirds of SME exporters are non-manufacturers.
- SMEs account for more than 93 percent of high-tech exporters.
- In 92 markets, SMEs are responsible for at least one-half of all U.S. exports.
- SMEs dominate exports to many smaller markets.

With the number of SMEs that are exporting at an all-time high, why is there a need for this book? Quite simply, because *the total number of SMEs exporting represent less than five percent of all SMEs in the United States!*

Why aren't more SMEs exporting? Two words: payment risk.

The exporter and importer often have conflicting goals, particularly when they are negotiating payment terms. The exporter wants assurance that the importer can pay and prefers to be paid when the goods are shipped. This is critical; few SMEs can afford the adverse financial impact of nonpayment from a foreign buyer. The importer, on the other hand, wants assurance that the exporter will perform as agreed and, therefore, wants to delay payment as long as possible. Proper use of international trade finance methods will alleviate these concerns for both the buyer and seller.

What This Book Is *Not*

There are many aspects to an international transaction, and this book covers only one of them—financing. If you are looking for information on marketing, distribution, or other issues concerning doing business in another country, you will find very limited information on the subject here. The U.S. Small Business Administration and the affiliated Small Business Development Centers have staff who can guide you on matters of logistics, sales, and regulation, among others. In addition, the publisher has a number of books on related topics, a few of which are listed below:

- *Inside the World's Export Credit Agencies*
- *Inside the World's Development Finance Institutions*
- *Selling Clean Energy Technology to the World*
- *Terrorism & Personal Security: Reducing Your Chances of Becoming a Target*
- *International Marketing Imperative*

B. Keep Your Eyes Open—Minimizing Commercial and Political Risk

So you've made the decision to export overseas. Perhaps you received an order from an overseas buyer. Maybe you concluded that your business would benefit from a diversified revenue base. Whichever the case, to some extent, you can treat the transaction the same way you would with an order from a domestic customer. You, however, have additional risks as well.

In this section, we will examine the risks that are common to domestic and foreign sales and then look at the risks that are unique to export transactions. The common risks are referred to as the *commercial risks* of a transaction. Risks that are unique to exporting are called *political risks*.

Remember, we are focused on the payment aspect of the transaction. There are logistical risks for exporting as well, but we will refer to them only in terms of their impact on facilitating or preventing payment.

Commercial Risks

For our purposes, we will define commercial risks as any event that prevents the buyer from paying or prevents the seller from delivering the product or service. Commercial risk does not include any governmental action that prevents the buyer from paying or the seller's ability to deliver.

A wide variety of options are available to the exporter and importer when negotiating payment terms for an export transaction. These options are shown in Exhibit 1.

Exhibit 1   Optimal Payment Option Balances Needs of Buyer and Seller

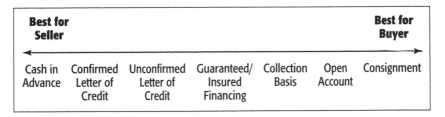

Best for Seller						Best for Buyer
Cash in Advance	Confirmed Letter of Credit	Unconfirmed Letter of Credit	Guaranteed/ Insured Financing	Collection Basis	Open Account	Consignment

Political Risk

Political risk involves the more institutional and unforeseen factors of transactions that may affect their outcome. Under political risk, the exporter and importer must evaluate how foreign country regulations, exchange controls, and political situations affect their activities.

The degree to which risk affects the exporter or importer is a direct result of the type of payment procedure employed and the arrangements made for implementing the transfer of goods and services. Commercial risk exposure shifts by degree between the exporter and importer, depending upon the type of payment procedure employed. Likewise, exposure to international risk is subject to the arrangements for payment and movement of goods and services.

Some examples of commercial risk are

- Problems with payment arrangements on behalf of the exporter/importer
- Problems with the merchandise on behalf of the exporter/importer
- Additional costs for financing, insurance, and shipping
- Additional costs for legal issues, redress, or adjustment

Some examples of political risk include:

- Problems with currency exchange
- Government or political intervention
- Problems with the movement of merchandise
- Unforeseen circumstances with the movement of merchandise or acts of God

Dealing with Commercial Risk

The best approach for dealing with commercial risk is to examine the potential risks with certain payment procedures (see Part I—Financing Short-Term Transactions). The risk exposure for each procedure is different for the exporter and importer. For the seller, the best protection against commercial risk exposure is a thorough credit examination of the potential buyer. This includes examining the buyer's credit history, focusing on ability to pay, amounts required to pay, and commitment to pay in a timely fashion. In turn, the buyer should question the seller's ability to ship the merchandise, integrity to fulfill obligation, and type of merchandise (quality and quantity) involved in the transaction.

Finding information to evaluate a potential buyer's or seller's credit history is a matter of examining banking, credit, and market information. Some potential sources of information are corporate reports, financial statements, buyer's/seller's banking and credit histories, credit services, and commercial credit reports.

Dealing with Political Risk

Because political risk involves exposure to the perils of international commerce and the domestic stability and policies of foreign countries, the buyer and seller can benefit greatly by examining readily available information on a particular country. In particular, prior to concluding a trade transaction, the buyer or seller should investigate the following:

- Current currency exchange controls in force
- Restrictions on importing or exporting merchandise
- A country's political and economic stability, including government policies toward imports, future trends, and foreign economic interests
- Known risks for methods of shipping

Sources for this type of information include:

- Embassies of a particular country
- Banks that operate internationally
- Trading services
- Published country and regional information such as the Economist Country Reports
- Experienced exporters that are familiar with a specific country or method of shipping

Protecting Against Buyer Risk

Although understanding the commercial and international risks inherent in trade transactions may reduce one's exposure to risk, such information does not provide complete protection against risk. Success in trade transactions requires having confidence that one be protected against risk. Insurance is available to mitigate risk exposure in international trade transactions. The Export-Import Bank of the United States (Ex-Im Bank) provides export credit insurance to protect U.S. exporters against nonpayment, political, and commercial risks. Similar agencies in a variety of countries provide export insurance for the same purpose. The Multilateral Investment Guarantee Agency (MIGA), an agency of the World Bank, offers long-term political risk insurance for international investments to complement national investment insurance programs, private insurance companies, and the International Finance Corporation (IFC). There are also a number of private insurance companies that provide U.S. exporters with coverage against losses due to nonpayment, commercial risks, and political risks.

C. International Trade Issues

Countries

There are over 180 different countries in the world, and each has its own traditions in conducting business and regulating international trade. Consequently, the exporters from one country must adapt their ways of trading to meet with those of another country. This requires the buyer or seller in a transaction to understand, or at least acknowledge, the differences in business practices and how they may affect international transactions. Conflicts may arise during a transaction that will require using knowledge and experience in how other countries conduct business.

Culture

Like the differences between countries, differences between cultures may seriously affect the outcome of a trade transaction. Considering the differences between cultures, including language and social customs, may be the determining factor for the success or failure of the deal.

Resources and Business Climate

The market potential and economic well-being of a country depends heavily upon a country's economic resources and business climate. The potential for exports, balance of payments, and foreign currency exchange are part of the larger economic picture. Tapping a lucrative market requires evaluating whether the business climate in a country is favorable. Some factors to examine when evaluating the business climate are per capita income, disposable wealth, sectors of economic strength and weakness, and economic trends.

Level of Development

Along with business climate, the level of development in a country may provide insight into the market potential for a specific country. Countries with lower levels of development may offer greater sales potential for certain economic sectors, such as improvements in transportation infrastructure or industrial development. At the same time, these countries may also have less stable markets, owing to rigid government economic policies, seasonal economic disasters like drought, or a host of other problems. More-developed countries may offer lucrative markets and have positive growth trends, but competition may also be fierce. It is important to evaluate carefully the level of economic development in relation to the market potential of doing business there.

Political Systems

A country's political system and stability may reflect upon its market potential and its business climate. The potential for serious political disorders, like war or strikes, may undermine economic stability and any attempts to do business in the country. In addition, political instability may also upset the economic system by sparking government intervention in the economy such as expropriation, restrictions against foreign investment, and importation regulations. Evaluating the political stability in a country is as important as measuring the economic stability and market potential.

Government Policies

A government may directly affect the business environment in a country by implementing its policies and via both the direct and subtle influence of government personnel. Directly, government policies may be restrictive toward international trade, limiting the repatriation of profits, imposing quotas upon the importation of certain commodities, or limiting foreign ownership or investment in a country. By contrast, government policies may lift restrictions to trade and imports, greatly enhancing international trade. Government personnel can be important factors in determining the outcome of government policies toward international trade. It is important to evaluate whether government personnel, as well as policies, are either supportive or restrictive toward international trade.

D. Recent Trends

The reality of globalization today is that, for U.S. companies, doing business in Singapore or Bangalore is only significantly different from doing business in San Francisco or New York by a few more hours in flight time. Recent books on the subject point to a flattened world where the Internet offers access to anyone with access to a computer and a phone line. Indeed, the days of international business as a separate functional discipline in operating companies are quickly becoming anachronistic. We no longer talk about interstate commerce, except in a legal sense. Selling products and services across state lines is just ordinary business. As the world's communication, transportation, and business infrastructures have improved, selling product across national borders has also become just plain old business.

Of course, there are still some very real differences in doing business across international borders, particularly in the area of finance. A U.S. company seeking to finance an account receivable from a company in California and from a company in India will find the two are treated very differently. The risks and the regulatory environment a lender faces on the Indian account receivable necessitate a very different approach. And when it comes to selling into more marginal (that is, riskier) markets, many of the same concerns are present that international traders have faced for centuries, going back to the days when letters of credit were first used in Italy.

Much news has circulated recently about the opportunities for U.S. business to expand into newly democratizing nations. Sad experience, however, has shown that the true foundation for a free market economy and prosperity is not achieved by merely holding elections. The following vignette provides an example of one company's difficulties operating in the international market. It should serve as a preemptive warning to U.S. firms thinking of investing in emerging markets swaddled in newly formed democracies supported by the U.S.

Pacific Island Aviation

Pacific Island Aviation (PIA), a U.S. 121–certificated-flag air carrier operating as a Northwest Airlines code share, launched a successful airline in the Caucuses region, Caucasus Airline (CA). They found out that, among others, the Azerbaijani government does not have to play by the rules, even with the U.S. government looking over its shoulder.

Caucasus Airline was a success story. As a small U.S. business, PIA launched a private, profitable, and locally run commercial airline between the Republics of Georgia, Azerbaijan, and Armenia. Capitalizing on the need for airline services for the oil companies, which are currently constructing pipelines from the Caspian Sea to Turkey, CA obtained backing from Lockheed Martin Air Traffic Management and a $4.6 million loan from the U.S. Overseas Private Investment Corporation (OPIC). Scheduled passenger service began November 2002, and load factors continued to grow according to plan. Routes expanded to Russia and the Ukraine, with charters flown throughout the region. Both the Georgian national carrier and another private airline discontinued service on CA's main routes, and this small, but tenacious, international aviation company eventually became successful enough to be viewed as a real competitor by the Azerbaijan airline—so successful, in fact, that senior Azerbaijani government officials decided to blatantly violate existing bilateral aviation treaties to cripple CA as a competitor.

Because CA's investment in Georgia had been underwritten, in part, by OPIC, CA expected that the U.S. government would be willing to warn the local authorities that such lawbreaking would not be tolerated. (In fact, one of the explicit reasons that CA and many other U.S. firms use OPIC investments is precisely because there is the implicit promise that the U.S. government will stand behind its investors when the going gets tough in these difficult markets.) No such firm warning was ever delivered to the Azerbaijani authorities because of stated "broader strategic interests."

This case study represents the risks inherent in conducting business in difficult markets, and although its purpose is meant to highlight legitimate concern when expanding overseas, the vast majority of overseas transactions provide a significant upside to U.S. businesses. The purpose of this book is to explain how to mitigate the risk in conducting international trade through the use of appropriate international finance tools.

E. Cross-Border Finance—The Current Environment

For small to medium size enterprises (SMEs), getting support with trade finance and competing on the international market can be very difficult. This is also true of larger firms with little or no international exposure. During the dot-com era, some rapidly growing firms believed they could conduct business overseas as they did from state to state in the United States. But, as much as globalization is shrinking the world, there are still a number of risks in selling overseas with which most U.S. lenders are uncomfortable. This is why the governments of a number of countries have created various programs to protect banks that extend credit across borders. The different types of Cross-Border Financing include the following:

- Bank–Government
- Bank–Bank
- Banks–Multinational Companies

- Banks–SME
- Multinational Companies–SME
- SME–SME

F. Principal Participants in International Trade Transactions

Commercial Banks

This is the largest financial sector in most countries. Commercial banks are usually short-term lenders. The principal international trade products that banks offer are loans, letters of credit, and documentary collections. Occasionally, banks will participate in medium-term export transactions, but this is usually in collaboration with government export credit agencies (ECAs) or multilateral organizations. Banks are normally interested in providing financial support in export transactions only to banks or government agencies. Private borrowers are not usually supported without a guarantee or aval of a local bank.

Finance Companies

These financial institutions are specialized lenders. Unlike banks, they do not take deposits and are not "full-service" financial institutions. Their funding is based on purchased money, which makes them more expensive than traditional banks. Many of these entities are owned by commercial banks. Finance companies are short-term lenders. They cannot issue or handle letters of credit, so their principal activity is making loans. There are very few finance companies that participate in international trade.

Factoring Companies

Similar to finance companies in that they are funded by purchased money, factoring companies are in the business of financing short-term exports. Many are owned and operated by banks. The only real difference between factoring companies and finance companies is that factors purchase accounts receivable without recourse, as opposed to just lending money secured by the receivable. There are very few international factoring companies.

Forfaiting Companies

Forfaiting companies are normally operated as subsidiaries of large international banks, mostly European. There are a few large U.S. banks that run forfaiting companies. Unlike commercial banks and other short-term lenders, forfaitors specialize in medium-term lending. Medium-term is defined as any transaction requiring financial support for between one and seven years. Because of the relatively narrow focus of forfaitors on capital equipment transactions, there are very few forfaiting companies.

Insurance Companies

Insurance companies offer insurance products for the international trade community. Most of their products are designed to protect receivables from default of any kind. This type of insurance is called credit risk insurance. Companies can insure against either commercial risks of loss or political risks. It is preferable, in most cases, to insure against both risks. Insurance policies have traditionally been harder to use as a financing instrument than, say, a guarantee. As a result, insurance has not been used as much as have loans and guarantees to finance international trade. This is rapidly changing, because the insurance industry has taken action in recent years to make their products more competitive and appealing to the business community. Insurance policies today are less restrictive and priced more competitively than they were just a few years ago.

The principal players in credit insurance are large private insurance companies and ECAs operated by governments around the world. Most credit insurance is used to support short-term receivables up to one year. Both private and government insurance companies offer this type of insurance. In medium-term transactions, government insurance programs offer most credit insurance.

Governments

All governments are involved in supporting international trade and investment. Trade and investment are considered the two key engines that drive economic growth. Governments set the tone for economic development through policy and actions. Most governments want to foster exports as opposed to imports. There is a widely held economic belief that exports foster internal job creation, whereas imports foster the export of jobs. As a result, most major economies have created specialized government institutions to help grow exports. Collectively, these are called export credit agencies (ECAs).

Export Credit Agencies

Governments fund these organizations to foster exports in their respective countries. The major Organization for Economic Cooperation and Development (OECD) countries operate the largest of these entities. In the

United States, this organization is called the Export-Import Bank (Ex-Im Bank). The ECAs of the OECD countries operate under uniform guidelines to assure a "level playing field" where companies compete on quality and price. There are occasions when a transaction is so important to the interests of a nation that their ECA offers a financing package that is designed to win the deal at all costs. This is called tied aid and is discouraged by OECD guidelines. The ECAs service exporters and banks and provide insurance programs, including medium-term loans and insurance, long-term loans, guarantees, and project finance.

Other Agencies

The ECAs are the dominant export promotion agencies. In many countries, however, specialty organizations are created to focus on specific needs. In the United States, there are a number of these entities. A few of them are highlighted below.

Overseas Private Investment Corporation

The Overseas Private Investment Corporation (OPIC) offers political risk insurance to U.S. investors, contractors, exporters, and financial institutions involved in international business in industrializing countries. Insurance is available for new ventures or expansions of existing enterprises and can cover equity investments, parent company and third party loans and guarantees, technical assistance agreements, cross-border leases, assigned inventory or equipment, as well as other forms of investment.

Commodity Credit Corporation

The Commodity Credit Corporation (CCC) offers financing programs to governments in developing countries to buy U.S. agricultural commodities. In some of these programs, financing can be arranged from one to three years. This allows countries in difficult financial conditions to buy foodstuffs and pay for them over a longer than normal period of time. Quotas are set each year by each country.

U.S. Small Business Administration

The U.S. Small Business Administration (SBA) offers loans to small companies. In recent years, the SBA has created small business loan programs for exporters. One of these programs was developed by the Ex-Im Bank and has been adapted for the SBA. It is called the Working Capital Guarantee Program, and it is designed to provide export working capital to small companies that might not normally have access to this type of program. Because the SBA is focused on small businesses, it wants to encourage these companies to export and offers export assistance programs to encourage involvement in the global market place.

In addition to the U.S. agencies listed above, the authors have contributed to other Thomson Publishing books that describe in detail the numerous government financing sources from around the world: *Inside the World's Development Finance Institutions* and *Inside the World's Export Credit Agencies.* These books can be a useful resource guide for transactions and projects in riskier markets.

PART I

FINANCING SHORT-TERM TRANSACTIONS

Ideally, companies would like to be paid in advance of providing goods and services—wouldn't we all. But unless your company produces something unique and necessary and there is essentially no competition, typically some type of vendor financing is part of doing business. Domestically, much of the business-to-business commerce is done on open account net 30-day terms after only the most cursory of credit checks. Frequently, of course, down payments are charged and, for larger purchases, a more thorough credit review is undertaken. This same approach is applied to international commerce, with many of the same financing tools that are used domestically. The main distinction, however, is that exporters typically put a higher value on obtaining more secure terms than they would for a domestic sale because of the risks—perceived or real.

The basic methods of payment for exports vary in terms of their attractiveness to the buyer and the seller, from cash in advance to open account or consignment selling. Neither of the extremes will be feasible for longer-term relationships, but they do have their use in certain situations. For example, in the 1999–2000 period, very few companies were exporting into Russia except on a cash-in-advance basis, owing to the country's financial turmoil. A marketer may use multiple methods of payment with the same buyer. For example, in a distributor relationship, the distributor may purchase samples on open account, but be required to pay for orders with a letter of credit.

Defining Methods of Payment (From Least to Most Risky)

There is always a pull between the two parties as to who will take on the risk in an international transaction—the buyer or the seller? On the one side of this graph, you have the importer taking complete risk by paying cash in advance for all goods or services. On the other, you have the exporter taking on the risk by giving the product in advance before any type of payment or guarantee of payment. Both extremes are hard to reach and should depend on the level of trust and risk in the importing and exporting countries. Because this book is written for the benefit of the exporter, we are assuming that the cash-in-advance option provides the least amount of risk,

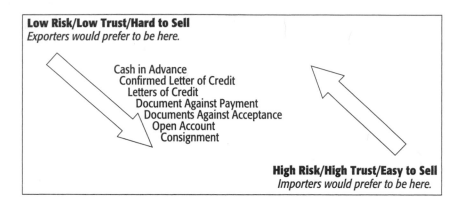

Low Risk/Low Trust/Hard to Sell
Exporters would prefer to be here.

Cash in Advance
Confirmed Letter of Credit
Letters of Credit
Document Against Payment
Documents Against Acceptance
Open Account
Consignment

High Risk/High Trust/Easy to Sell
Importers would prefer to be here.

whereas the consignment option is the riskiest. Most often, for the benefit of exporters and importers, one of the middle-of-the-road options will be reached so that risk can be shared through lending and financing institutions.

For exporters, risk is not only a function of the importer's ability/willingness to pay but also involves other risks outside its control, including:

- Political security
- Risks in shipping process
- Value of currency

Export credit terms add another dimension to the profitability of an export transaction. The exporter has, in all likelihood, already formulated a credit policy that determines the degree of risk the firm is willing to assume and the preferred selling terms. The main objective is to meet the importer's requirements without jeopardizing the firm's financial goals. The exporter will be concerned about being paid for the goods shipped and will, therefore, consider the following factors in negotiating terms of payment: (1) the amount of payment and the need for protection, (2) terms offered by competitors, (3) practices in the industry, (4) capacity for financing international transactions, and (5) relative strength of the parties involved. If the exporter is well established in the market with a unique product and accompanying service, price and terms of trade can be set to fit the exporter's desires. If, on the other hand, the exporter is breaking into a new market or if competitive pressures call for action, pricing and selling terms should be used as major competitive tools. Both parties have their own concerns and sensitivities; therefore, this very basic issue should be put on the negotiating table at the very beginning of the relationship.

Questions to Ask Before Selecting the Payment Method

The most beneficial type of financing for the exporter depends on the specific characteristics of the exporter itself, the transaction, and the importer. By answering some simple questions, including those listed below, exporters can assess their risk tolerance objectively. Thus, the correct payment method can be established to balance the needs of minimizing financial risks yet maximizing the transaction's profitability.

- Can the business afford the loss if it is not paid?
- Will extending credit and the possibility of waiting several months for payment still make the sale profitable?
- Can the sale be made only by extending credit?
- How long have the buyers been operating, and what is their credit history?
- Are there reasonable alternatives for collecting if the buyers do not meet their obligations? (That is, does the buyer's country have the legal and business infrastructure for settling transaction disputes fairly and swiftly?)
- If shipments are made but not accepted, can alternative buyers be found?

CHAPTER 1

CASH IN ADVANCE

What Is It?

This payment procedure requires the buyer of goods or services to pay the manufacturer or seller prior to receiving the merchandise. Upon receiving payment, the seller ships the merchandise to the buyer via a prearranged method of transport. This procedure involves very little risk on the part of the seller. The seller has no obligation to send the merchandise unless payment is received, and there is no obligation for the seller to present the merchandise to the buyer for inspection. Exporters seldom employ this procedure as importers often consider it too risky.

A variation on this theme would be to require a partial up-front payment or down payment. This is a very common approach on larger-value transactions, particularly when contracts are involved. For example, as a matter of policy, ECAs routinely require 15 percent down payments by the importer for capital equipment purchases. Progress payments on larger transactions often include acceptance requirements by the purchaser before payment is made. In the case of these types of advance payments, it is important to note that the importer may be uncomfortable providing the advance without the exporter posting a reciprocal standby letter of credit.

Although we will be discussing letters of credit later, the posting of a standby letter of credit gives importers comfort that if the merchandise is not delivered as agreed, they can get their money back by drawing funds from the letter of credit. (The trigger is usually a nonperformance issue on the part of the seller.) The net effect of posting a standby letter of credit from the exporter's perspective is that it does not enjoy the benefit of cash flow from the advance payment. It only enjoys the security of knowing the money is "in the bank." This is particularly the case for smaller businesses, which typically need to collateralize a standby letter of credit with cash in the same amount.

With cash in advance for the entire transaction amount, the buyers expose themselves to considerable risk. There is no obligation for the seller to send the merchandise, because the seller has already received payment for the goods. In addition, the buyer has no way to verify that the goods purchased represent the quality and quantity ordered. The buyer relies solely upon the seller's integrity to provide the merchandise as arranged. Because of the required level of trust, this method of payment is usually employed by importers who do not have a well-established relationship with exporters or for purchasing a small amount of goods, such as product samples.

Knowing the seller is the fundamental requirement for buyers choosing to pay in advance for goods and services. This requires examining the seller's credit history, business integrity, and potential means to redress any grievances with the seller before submitting payment.

Players/Process

- Buyer pays via wire transfer, check, draft, or credit card
- Seller ships

The most favorable term to the exporter is cash in advance because it relieves the exporter of all risk and allows for immediate use of the money. It is not widely used, however, except for smaller, first-time transactions or situations in which the exporter has reason to doubt the importer's ability to pay. Cash-in-advance terms are also found when orders are for custom-made products, because the risk to the exporter is beyond that of a normal transaction. In some instances, the importer may not be able to buy on a cash-in-advance basis because of insufficient funds or government restrictions.

Wire Transfers

For high-risk or first-transaction situations or when documentary collections or letters of credit cannot be negotiated, there is a hybrid sort of term falling somewhere between open account and absolute payment in advance, yet safer in many situations than documents against payment. We refer to wire transfer payments between banks on notification of the arrival of the merchandise at the dock of embarkation. A dock receipt can be issued for proof, if necessary, and the buyer's agent can even be invited to examine the goods before they are loaded aboard ship. Other variations can call for wire transfer at the time of shipment or some other trigger, but these latter variations become a matter of timing rather than risk abatement because, in these cases, the merchandise is irretrievably bound for an overseas destination.

CHAPTER 2

LETTERS OF CREDIT

What Are They?

A letter of credit (LC) is a document issued by a bank to carry out a buyer's or importer's specific instructions regarding a trade transaction. The LC specifies the nature of the trade transaction to be conducted, including the dates and destination for shipping merchandise, the necessary documents to be sent by the seller, the method of payment, dates by which the transaction should be completed, and the conditions the seller must satisfy to receive payment. These detailed instructions usually follow a standard format described in the Uniform Customs and Practices (UCP) for Documentary Credits, International Chamber of Commerce (ICC) Publication Number 500, known as UCP 500 (see Appendix for this document).

The major parties of LC transactions are the buyer (Applicant) and seller (Beneficiary) and their respective banks acting on their behalf. The issuing bank issues the LC and acts on behalf of the buyer. The advising bank acts on behalf of the beneficiary by being the financial agent for the seller, verifying the documents, authorizing the payment to the seller (if authorized), and submitting the documents to the issuing bank. The relationship between the buyer and seller and their respective banks under an LC provides the buyer and seller with additional protection against commercial and international risks. For the buyer using an LC substitutes the creditworthiness of the issuing bank for his own. For the seller, this substitution reduces the risk of nonpayment because banks commit themselves to pay if the seller's documents are correct. The seller also gains by being protected against the buyer's possible rejection of the merchandise, because the issuing bank has assured payment to the seller if he/she fulfills the terms of the letter. The buyer has no right to inspect the merchandise under an LC. The role of the banks involved is solely to review the documents required by the LC. They do not concern themselves with the quality or the nature of the merchandise being shipped. Payment is assured to the seller if the documents are in order. Consequently, the buyer has no recourse to prevent payment if the documents are in order.

The LC payment method principally provides protection for the seller against payment risk. To assure himself of this risk protection, the seller must

20

completely fulfill the terms of the LC. For the buyer, once an LC has been successfully performed, the payment obligation must be honored. The buyer's risk is that the supplier never ships the merchandise or ships unacceptable or inferior merchandise. Both parties in the transaction benefit by using LCs in precise and well-defined transactions. Letters of credit should be well-defined, written clearly, and understood by both parties prior to engaging in the transaction to avoid risk at a later stage.

Various Characteristics of Letters of Credit

Irrevocable

An *irrevocable* LC cannot be "revoked or cancelled" unilaterally by any party once it has been issued, unless all of the parties involved agree to the "revocation/cancellation" in writing. This is an important aspect of an LC because it protects the seller, and it is recommended that all LCs be irrevocable.

Revocable

The opposite is a *revocable* LC. This type of LC can be canceled by the issuing bank at any time without the permission of other parties. Consequently, a revocable LC is seldom used in international trade transactions. To be revocable, an LC must state that it is revocable. If the LC does not state it is revocable, it is by definition irrevocable.

Confirmed

A *confirmed* LC has the backing of another bank besides that of the issuing bank. The confirming bank adds its credit backing to that of the issuing bank to assure payment on the LC. Should the issuing bank have difficulty paying an LC, the confirming bank would be responsible for payment.

Unconfirmed

An *unconfirmed* LC does not have the payment assurance of another bank. It stands solely on the credit standing of the issuing bank. Before accepting an unconfirmed LC, a beneficiary should carefully examine the credit history and business integrity of the issuing bank, and the political risks in its country.

An *advising* bank is responsible for transmitting the LC to the beneficiary and verifying its authenticity. It should be noted that the advising bank is not the same as a confirming bank, although the same bank may have both roles.

Straight

A *straight* LC requires the beneficiary to present documents and to request payment at the counters of a specific bank. No other bank may be used to negotiate documents.

Negotiable

A *negotiable* LC allows the beneficiary to employ any bank as its intermediary to examine documents and request payment, even if this bank is not the advising bank. This bank can, at its sole discretion, pay the beneficiary, provided that the beneficiary fulfills the terms of the credit and all commercial documents are in order.

Sight

A *sight* LC requires the banks to provide payment to the beneficiary immediately after determining compliance of the necessary commercial documents. The only acceptable delay to a sight credit is if a reimbursing bank is employed for payment. This delay is usually only a matter of one day to a few days.

Usance

A *usance* LC is one that calls for a payment at a future date rather than at sight. Under this type of LC, usance (time) drafts will be presented with the required documents. If the documents comply with the LC terms, the draft is "honored" by the drawee bank by "accepting" it for payment at the specified future date. Because the accepted draft is a negotiable instrument, it has an additional advantage to the beneficiary. The beneficiary may elect to receive funds prior to the draft maturity date by requesting the drawee/accepting bank to pay the draft amount on a "discounted" basis.

Should the parties of a transaction not want to use time drafts as the negotiable payment tool, the issuing bank may issue a *deferred payment* LC. The methodology in this type of LC is the same as described under usance drafts but does not involve the use of negotiable instruments (drafts). The disadvantage to the beneficiaries of this arrangement is that they cannot receive payment at the time of presenting documents. They must wait until the deferred payment period has ended.

Transferable

A *transferable* LC allows the beneficiary the right to transfer the proceeds of an LC to another person(s) or beneficiaries. This additional beneficiary becomes a party to the terms and conditions of the credit. The credit may be transferred as a whole or in parts to different persons and may involve a complete transfer or only a partial transfer. An LC can be transferred only once. It may not be retransferred. Most LCs issued today are in payment for goods shipped or services performed. Payment is normally made against documents consisting of commercial invoices, packing lists, certificates of origin, and shipping documents for goods shipped. Payment for services may be against invoices, vouchers, paid bills, or other records of work performed. Letters of credit of this nature are usually referred to as *merchandise or documentary* credits. These are "active instruments," which means they are meant to be used as the "principal" means of payment.

Standby

Standby is a term used for LCs that function like insurance. These types of LCs are "passive." That is, they are not to be drawn upon by the beneficiary unless a delinquency/default of some form takes place in a business transaction. Standby LCs are usually substituted for a guarantee or bond in the United States.

Standby LCs issued by U.S. banks are subject to federal law, specifically, Regulation H (12 CFR 203). Under section 208.8 (d), a standby LC is defined as follows:

> *"Standby Letters of Credit include every letter of credit (or similar arrangement, however named or designated) which represents an obligation to the beneficiary on the part of the issuer (1) to repay money borrowed by or advanced to or for the account of the account party, or (2) to make payment on account of any evidence of indebtedness by the account party, or (3) to make payment on account of any default by the account party in the performance of an obligation."*

Even though Standby LCs are covered under federal law, in practice, U.S. banks apply the UCP 500 and/or the International Standby Practices (ISBP) to the issuance of Standby LCs for the support of international trade transactions.

Players/Process

The four major parties of an LC are the buyer, the issuing bank, the advising bank, and the beneficiary. Their roles in the transaction are:

- The **buyer,** commonly called the "account party," submits an application requesting an LC with specific instructions on how to proceed with the LC.

- The **beneficiary** is also the seller who, by accepting the LC sent to him/her, must agree to its terms and conditions. The terms of an LC usually require shipping goods or services and submitting the necessary commercial and financial documents to the banks involved with the LC. Once all obligations have been fulfilled, the beneficiary receives payment for his/her merchandise as stated in the LC.
- The **issuing bank** issues the LC. By doing so, the issuing bank substitutes its credit risk for that of the buyer. Once issued, the bank makes itself responsible for the payment outlined in the LC.
- The **advising bank** receives the LC, verifies its authenticity, and delivers it to the beneficiary. It is common for the advising bank to be a correspondent bank of the issuing bank.

Other possible parties to an LC transaction:

- The **paying bank** is authorized to pay the LC to the beneficiary. There is always a paying bank in every LC. It is beneficial to the U.S. seller to have the advising bank be the paying bank rather than the issuing. This will usually speed up the payment process by a number of days to a number of weeks. The seller must request this transaction structure with the buyer before the LC is issued. In an LC that requires drafts to be presented for payment, the seller wants the advising bank to also be the "drawee" bank. In this case, the advising and paying bank are one and the same.
- A **confirming bank** is a third party bank, which, if requested by the issuing bank, can add its payment commitment/assurance to the LC. This payment commitment/assurance may be recommended if there are uncertainties about the issuing bank's credit history or the country conditions in the issuing bank's country. It is common for the confirming bank and the advising bank to be the same institution.
- A **reimbursing bank** may be solicited by the issuing bank to provide payment to the paying/confirming or negotiating bank once an LC has been fulfilled and payment approved. This usually occurs when the issuing bank does not have an account with the advising or confirming bank.
- A **negotiating bank** facilitates the process of document compliance, examination, and draft payment. Usually, beneficiaries want to select a negotiating bank to act on their behalf.

Steps of an LC

1. The buyer and seller agree on terms for a transaction. These terms may be written as an informal or formal sales contract. Because the seller is the beneficiary, he/she must negotiate the terms of the LC wisely. The seller should never let the buyer control the terms and conditions of the LC. What is the reason for this? The LC is supposed to protect the seller financially. If the buyer wants protection, he/she should not agree to the LC payment method.

2. Agreeing to use an LC as the payment procedure, the buyer applies to his/her bank for the LC. Following the LC's terms it negotiated with the seller, the buyer requests the beneficiary in the LC to provide necessary commercial documents in return for payment. The "necessary" commercial documents should only be those that the buyer needs for customs clearance in its country.

3. After issuing the credit, the issuing bank either selects a bank, usually a correspondent bank located near the beneficiary, or uses a bank requested by the beneficiary to advise the letter to the beneficiary.

4. Either the advising bank or another bank may add its "confirmation" to the LC if requested to do so by the issuing bank, replacing the issuing bank's commitment to make payment upon completion of the credit's terms. It is the seller/beneficiary that determines whether or not the LC should be confirmed and requests this of the buyer when they negotiate the "terms" of the LC.

5. The beneficiary chooses to either accept or reject the LC's terms. If he/she accepts, the beneficiary prepares the merchandise for shipment and the necessary commercial documents. If the beneficiary rejects the LC, he/she must notify both the advising bank and the buyer that he/she does not plan to use the LC. It is unusual for LCs to be rejected outright by sellers. A more normal occurrence finds the seller requesting changes/amendments to the original LC so that the modified form meets his/her needs. Any and all changes/modifications/amendments to an original LC must be requested through the buyer.

6. After shipment, the beneficiary presents commercial documents and possibly a draft to the advising, negotiating, paying, or confirming bank for examination of the documents.

7. The bank that examines the documents verifies that they are correct according to the LC's terms and, if correct, may elect to pay the beneficiary.

8. The advising, negotiating, paying, or confirming bank seeks payment from the issuing bank and sends the commercial documents for further review to the issuing bank. When there is a negotiating, paying, or confirming bank, the documents are normally reviewed by the issuing bank only after a payment has already been made to the beneficiary.

9. The issuing bank reviews the commercial documents. If in order, the bank debits the account of the buyer, transfers title to the merchandise in transit if assigned to the bank, and releases the documents to the buyer to collect the merchandise. The issuing bank, if it has not already done so, must immediately submit payment to the advising, negotiating, confirming, or reimbursing bank.

- Issuing bank opens LC on behalf of buyer
- Issuing bank forwards LC to seller's bank
- Seller's bank advises LC to the seller
- Seller agrees to the LC terms
- Seller ships and sends documents to its bank
- Bank examines documents
- If documents are correct it may pay seller
- Seller's bank seeks reimbursement from IB

Rules/Documentation Needed

The format for the issuance of LCs in the United States is specified both by the U.S. Department of the Treasury and the Comptroller of the Currency (Interpretative Rulings, May 5, 1977. Section 7.7016–Letters of Credit). These Rulings state:

> *"A national bank may issue letters of credit permissible under the Uniform Commercial Code or the Uniform Customs and Practice for Documentary Credits to or on behalf of its customers. As a matter of sound banking practice, letters of credit should be issued in conformity with the following: (a) Each LC should be conspicuously entitled as such. (b) The bank's undertaking should contain a specified expiration date or be for a definite term. (c) The bank's undertaking should be limited in amount. (d) The bank's obligation to pay should arise only upon the presentation of a draft or other documents as specified in the LC, and the bank must not be called upon to determine questions of fact or law at issue between the account party and the beneficiary. (e) The bank's customer should have an unqualified obligation to reimburse the bank for payments made under the LC."*

The preceding format, although specifically for U.S. banks, is a concept that is generally followed throughout the world. Both merchandise and standby LCs must conform to this format. This format is an integral part of the UCP 500, the standard by which LCs are transacted throughout the world.

Important Clauses of an LC

International LCs should always be subject to the most recent version of the UCP for Documentary Credits of the ICC. The current is the UCP 500, 1993 revision. In the United States, banks may issue LCs subject to the Uniform Commercial Code, as applied by each state; however, this is not common practice.

Some examples of legal clauses are:

• This letter of credit is subject to the Uniform Customs and Practices for Documentary Credits (1993 Revision, International Chamber of Commerce, Paris, France, Publication No. 500).
• This letter of credit is subject to the Uniform Commercial Code of the Commonwealth of Pennsylvania.

Legal opinions concur that there is no conflict between the Uniform Commercial Code and UCP for Documentary Credits. The UCP 500 clause only expounds or details the general principals for LCs under the Uniform Commercial Code. At times, if the beneficiary and/or account party insist, both clauses may appear without conflict; however, in international trade, the global practice is to only apply the UCP 500 to LCs.

Shipping and Expiration Dates

The LC details the required method of shipping for the merchandise and the date for presentation of documents. Also, the location where the document presentation is to take place is usually stated. For straight LCs, this location would normally be the counters of the issuing bank, unless otherwise stated. It is important for the exporter to recognize any time constraints in preparing the documents for presentation by the date stated. For example, obtaining an ocean bill of lading may take up to 10 days, which could impose serious time constraints on the exporter to fulfill the letter's terms.

Although not required in an LC, shipping dates for merchandise are typically included and should not occur any later than 25–30 days prior to the LC's expiration date. If not stated, the goods may be shipped at any time, but the required documents should be presented prior to the expiration date.

The standard period for presenting documents is 21 days after the ship date. Documents older than 21 days, unless otherwise stated, are generally considered invalid.

Special Clauses

The *Red Clause* is an uncommon addition to an LC, allowing the beneficiary to receive pre-shipment advances, with the buyer's faith that the exporter will fulfill the terms of the letter. The red clause is accompanied by a statement that the necessary commercial documents will be provided at a specific date. A red clause LC allows a beneficiary to borrow money from the advising bank on the understanding that the amount of the advance, including interest, will be deducted from the total proceeds of the LC when the beneficiary requests payment under the LC.

Food and Drug clauses allow payment to the beneficiary only after obtaining written certification from the relevant government agencies that the merchandise has been inspected and approved. This clause is a specific notice for exporters to obtain the necessary commercial documents for merchandise that may require special certification for export. For example, a country's import restriction may require that food products have a specific purity level, requiring the exporter to provide documents showing compliance with these regulations. It is important for the buyer to use this clause if there are potential restrictions on exporting that may delay shipment.

Revolving Letter of Credit clauses specify how an LC may become an on-going, repetitive exporting process. The revolving clauses detail how a credit may be replenished once a transaction is completed and payment is made. The clauses also specify the time frame in which this replenishment process can occur. This process is useful for exporters who have a close relationship with their buyers and who deal in a steady flow of exports to them. It is important for the parties of a credit to clarify whether the revolving credit is automatic or requires approval to begin a new credit cycle.

Jenner Jahn Machine Company

Jenner Jahn Machine Company (JJM) had a dilemma. It had an opportunity to sell a $600,000 piece of equipment to a company in Serbia and Montenegro, but it could not get the Serbian company to agree to a cash-in-advance transaction. The buyer did not have the cash, but it had arranged financing from a bank in Serbia. As a small family-run business, JJM did not want to take any buyer payment risk. In this case, the best payment alternative was an LC, which the buyer offered to do. Jenner Jahn Machine, however, had never completed an LC before. Although the transaction needed to get done quickly, the most common mistake of exporters is to proceed with the LC transaction by letting the buyer set up the LC. This can allow the buyer to prepare the LC with unfavorable conditions for the seller/beneficiary.

Fortunately, JJM had prepared itself by attending a specialized Trade Finance seminar offered by one of the authors. Not feeling comfortable negotiating with the buyer alone, JJM contracted consulting services from the author. The transaction began in earnest at the beginning of December 2003. Owing to the proximity of the holidays, it was concluded that shipment had to be made in early January to avoid any problems. The LC terms and conditions were negotiated and finalized in under three weeks. The time line for performance was very tight. It was agreed that the LC needed to be issued within the first two weeks of January and it expired on the 15th of February. These dates created a lot of pressure on JJM to prepare the logistical and documentary aspects of the sale very promptly. This required active discussions with their freight forwarder and banker. Nervous, but confident that the LC terms were negotiated in its favor, JJM was ready to execute the transaction.

The buyer held up its end of the deal by getting the LC issued on January 12, 2004. And JJM's bank received the LC and advised it to the company the same day. Working carefully with their freight forwarder, JJM had the machine shipped (loaded on board a vessel bound for Europe) on January 18. Within two days, they had procured the bill of lading and had prepared all of their documents and presented them via courier to their bank. The bank knew this was an important transaction for JJM, so they promptly reviewed the documents within two days and, because they were the confirming bank, JJM received its funds within four days because this was the agreed upon payment delay built into the LC.

What was the result? Jenner Jahn Machine successfully shipped its machine to the buyer under a well-structured LC and received all of its funds within eight days of shipment! The lesson is clear: LCs can be very efficient payment tools if negotiated properly.

Engagement Clauses

Through the Engagement Clause, banks assume the obligation and the liability for payment or acceptance if the beneficiary meets the terms and conditions of the LC.

For Straight Letters of Credit

The following clauses are used primarily with domestic, bond, or standby LCs:

- "All drafts drawn under and in conformity with the terms of this credit will be duly honored upon delivery of documents as specified if presented at this office on or before (expiration date of letter of credit)."
- "We engage with you that all drafts drawn under and in compliance with the terms of this credit will be duly honored upon presentation (plus expiration date clause)."
- "The above mentioned correspondent engages with you that all drafts drawn under and in compliance with the terms of this advice will be duly honored upon presentation (plus expiration date clause)."

For Negotiable LCs

The following clauses are used primarily with negotiable LCs:

- "We hereby agree with the drawers, endorsers, and bona fide holders of drafts drawn under and in compliance with the terms of this credit that such drafts will be duly honored upon presentation."
- "We hereby agree with you and negotiating banks or bankers that if drafts are presented in compliance with the terms of this credit that such drafts shall be duly honored on due presentation to the drawee."
- "The above mentioned correspondent engages with you and negotiating banks or bankers that drafts in compliance with the terms of this credit shall be duly honored on due presentation to the drawee."
- "The above mentioned correspondent agrees with the drawers, endorsers, and bona fide holders of drafts drawn under and in compliance with the terms of this credit that such drafts will be duly honored upon presentation."

The preceding standard negotiation clauses will appear in the LC; however, additional clauses must be added for restricting the negotiation. Some examples include:

- "Negotiations are to be made only at the office of . . ."
- "Negotiations under this Letter of Credit are restricted to . . ."

Some examples of clauses concerning the charges for negotiation include:

- "Negotiation charges are for your account."
- "Negotiation charges are for the account of the beneficiary."
- "Negotiation charges are for the buyer's account."
- "Negotiation charges are for the account party in this credit."

Note: When the LC is silent about negotiation charges, it is presumed that the charges will be for the beneficiary's account, if a drawee bank is named. If no drawee bank is named, the opposite is true.

For Confirmed and Unconfirmed LCs

The clause "We hereby confirm the above letter of credit and undertake that all drafts drawn and presented as above specified will be duly honored by us" is used primarily with confirmed LCs, whereas the clause "All drafts, with documents as specified, must be presented at this office not later than (expiration date of letter of credit)" is used primarily with unconfirmed LCs.

LC Flow Chart

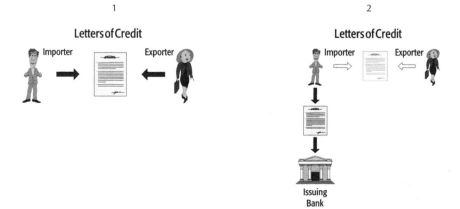

3

Letters of Credit

4

Letters of Credit

5

Letters of Credit

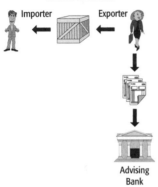

6

Letters of Credit

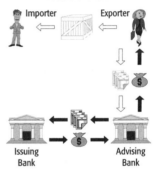

7

Letters of Credit

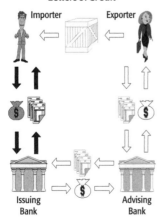

Disadvantages of the LC

Although the LC can serve to distribute risk between the buyer and seller evenly, the intent of an LC is to principally provide protection to the seller. It is up to the seller to know how to properly negotiate the terms of an LC. If he/she does so correctly, the seller truly is the "beneficiary" in the transaction, not just in "name" but in actuality. The LC presents its own disadvantages however. If even the smallest discrepancies exist in the timing of manufacturing, shipment, the presentation of documents, or other requirements of the LC, the buyer can reject the shipment and its payment obligation to the issuing bank. Some statistics show that nearly 50 percent of submissions for LC payment are initially rejected for failure to comply with terms![2] For example, if the terms require the delivery of four specific documents and one of them is incomplete or delivered late, then the buyer has sufficient grounds to withhold payment or reject shipment even if every other condition was fulfilled and the shipment arrived in perfect order. Therefore, the seller must negotiate the LC terms carefully, consider all the details before accepting an LC, and be certain that the details are followed stringently. The following table provides the most common discrepancies that cause nonpayments of LCs:[3]

Common Discrepancies That Cause Nonpayments of LCs

General
1. Documents inconsistent with each other
2. Description of goods on invoice differs from that in the credit
3. Marks and numbers differ between the documents
4. Absence of documents called for in the credit
5. Incorrect names and addresses

Drafts (Bill of Exchange)
1. Amount does not match invoice
2. Drawn on wrong party
3. Not endorsed correctly
4. Drawn payable on an indeterminable date

(Continued)

---

2 Giovannucci, Daniele. "Payment Methods in International Trade." World Bank. 1999. Accessed from lnweb18.worldbank.org/essd/essd.nsf/0/37343b58a4cf229c852568ae0012cbff/$FILE/Trade%20Finance%20Tools.pdf in July 2005.

3 Ibid.

Common Discrepancies That Cause Nonpayments of LCs (*Continued*)

Transport Documents

1. Shipment made between ports other than those stated in the credit
2. Signature on bill of lading does not specify on whose behalf it was signed
3. Required number of originals not presented
4. Bill of lading does not evidence whether freight is prepaid or collect
5. No evidence of goods actually "shipped on board"
6. Bill of lading incorrectly consigned

Insurance

1. Insurance document presented of a type other than that required by the credit
2. Shipment is underinsured
3. Insurance not effective for the date in the transport documents
4. Insurance policy is incorrectly endorsed

Deadlines

1. Late shipment
2. Late presentation of documents
3. Credit expired

CHAPTER 3

DOCUMENTARY COLLECTIONS

What Are They?

Documentary collections are a payment procedure based upon specific instructions received by banks from the seller involved in a trade transaction. The two types of collections are:

- **Documents Against Payment** (D/P), involving the receipt of funds from the buyer by a bank in exchange for the transfer of documents to the buyer
- **Documents Against Acceptance** (D/A), involving the acceptance of drafts or bills of exchange by the buyer in exchange for the transfer of commercial documents to the buyer

Documentary collections represent a payment procedure that is more balanced in favor of the buyer, wherein the buyer only has to make payment once he/she knows that the product has arrived and the required customs clearance documents are at a bank in the buyer's country. The buyer only receives the merchandise after he/she makes payment to the bank (Cash Against Documents) or makes a commitment, in writing, to pay at some definite future date (Documents Against Acceptance). This procedure involves the seller undertaking the shipment of merchandise to the buyer; but before taking control of the merchandise, the buyer must receive authorized documents from the seller. These documents represent authorization from the seller to the shipping company holding the merchandise to transfer authority to the buyer. The seller will provide these documents to the buyer via a third-party financial institution, known as a collecting bank. Usually in the buyer's country, the collecting bank acts on behalf of the seller, receiving the documents, notifying the buyer that it is holding the documents, and, only upon receipt of payment from the buyer or after "acceptance" of the seller's draft by the buyer, providing the documents to the buyer.

Collection documents typically include either straight or negotiable bills of lading together with other standard documents including, but not limited to, an invoice, packing list, certificate of origin, and insurance certificate. From the exporter's point of view, the use of documentary collections provides less payment security than with letters of credit. Therefore, it is extremely important to never consign the bills of lading directly to the buyer or their freight forwarder. Documentary collections split the risk involved in the transaction more evenly between the buyer and seller than with letters of credit; however, the major risks are still borne by the seller. The seller's principal risk is the buyer's rejection of merchandise and nonpayment. Both actions require the seller to dispose of the merchandise and assume losses from the costs of shipping and delays. The seller retains valuable financial leverage in the transaction, however, because the buyer must provide a payment or an acceptance against receiving the documents. The buyer's principal risk is that the merchandise is not the quality or quantity ordered. When the collecting bank receives the documents, it does not investigate whether the documents accurately represent the quality and quantity of the merchandise. The collecting bank only acts as a custodian of the documents until the buyers consummates their side of the transaction. Customs regulations or government confiscation may also delay the buyer's assuming authority over the merchandise.

Knowing the credit history and business integrity is vital for both the buyer and seller, who must risk receiving unsatisfactory merchandise or its rejection, respectively. It is also important to investigate the trading regulations and restrictions for a particular country to avoid any delays with customs or the seizure of the merchandise.

Players/Process

The principal parties in a collection procedure:

- The **principal/drawer** is the seller or exporter in a transaction who initiates the collection process by drawing a draft on the buyer.
- The **drawee** is the buyer or importer on whom a draft is drawn and payment is expected.
- The drawer's bank, which is entrusted to deliver commercial documents to the buyer's country, is known as the **remitting bank**.
- Any bank in the buyer's country, which the seller uses to receive documents, is known as the **collecting bank**.
- The **presenting bank** is the collecting bank that eventually submits to the buyer a draft for acceptance or documents for payment. In most transactions, the collecting bank and the presenting bank are the same.

General Documentary Collections Process

- Seller ships
- Seller presents documents to seller's bank
- Bank sends documents to a correspondent
- Correspondent bank releases documents against buyer's payment/acceptance
- Correspondent wires funds to seller's bank
- Seller's bank pays seller

Documents Against Payment Process

The Documents Against Payment (D/P) collection process is initiated by the exporter as part of a trade transaction. The D/P process proceeds as follows:

1. The exporter, or drawer, draws a bank draft on the buyer or drawee for the sales amount of the ordered merchandise in the transit process.
2. This draft is sent by the exporter through the remitting bank to a foreign bank, either the collecting bank or presenting bank, along with commercial documents such as a bill of lading for the merchandise in transit.
3. Once the documents and draft are in the presenting bank's possession, the importer may submit payment to the bank, which, in turn, sends the payment to the exporter's bank and releases the commercial documents to the importer or drawee.
4. With the commercial documents, the importer can obtain the merchandise upon its arrival.

It is important to note that until the drawee pays the draft amount and receives the commercial documents, the exporter should retain both title and control over the merchandise in transit. Should any problem arise once the documents have been exchanged for payment, sellers may investigate the whereabouts of the funds or documents by requesting an advice of fate from their remitting bank. An advice of fate is the process of tracing the funds and documents should any problems with payment occur. It is also important that the drawer need not use a remitting bank to send the commercial documents to a collecting bank. The drawer may prepare the documents and send them, thus saving the costs of remittance fees. If the seller decides to omit the services of the remitting bank, it assumes more risk because it eliminates the collection clout of the remitting bank if problems arise. For the small remittance fee involved, it is generally advisable to use a remitting bank.

Although this payment procedure offers some protection against risk for both the buyer and seller, the latter still faces considerable risk that the importer may not provide payment in exchange for the commercial documents. This is, in effect, the buyer's rejection of the merchandise, also known as a nonpayment. In this situation, the exporter has no recourse against the buyer. The exporter's only option is to dispose of the merchandise to cover product costs and freight charges. The presenting bank has no responsibility for the buyer accepting the merchandise. It is solely responsible for notifying the buyer of the collection process. In the event of a nonpayment, the exporter has the option to protest, which the presenting bank undertakes on his/her behalf. This procedure is not recommended unless the nonpayment is something the exporter is willing to take to court. A nonpayment may result from a delay in transit, so any formal protest may seriously upset relations between the buyer and seller.

It is advantageous for the exporter to have sound information on the credit history and business integrity of both the buyer and the presenting bank before entering into a trade transaction. The seller might also use the buyer's primary bank as a presenting bank because it may have some leverage over the buyer in the event of a nonpayment.

Documents Against Payment collections are commonly used only for transactions involving shipments by sea. This is because of the differences in documentation between ocean bills of lading and air waybills. Unlike ocean bills of lading, air waybills are nonnegotiable and, frequently, the importer's name is used as the recipient for the merchandise. This increases the risk for the seller that the importer might obtain the merchandise before payment is received. To prevent this, the seller and buyer can agree to have a third party, such as the presenting bank or a shipping agent, named as the recipient on air waybills. This party would transfer authority over the merchandise once payment is received.

For exporters using D/Ps frequently that involve merchandise in small volumes or amounts, it may be advantageous to use a short-cut procedure as a way to avoid remitting bank fees. Exporters may avoid using the remitting bank to process documentary collections by submitting the necessary documents and draft to a presenting bank themselves. This procedure is worthwhile for small transactions, yet still retains the protection against risk provided by D/Ps.

Documents Against Acceptance Process

The Documents Against Acceptance procedure for collections is identical to the Documents Against Payment procedure, with the exception of payment method. Instead of providing a draft with commercial documents against payment, the exporter submits a time draft with extended payment terms.

This is a form of promissory note stating that the drawee/signatory agrees to pay within a certain number of days after accepting the draft, usually a period of 30–180 days. When the buyer signs (accepts) the draft in order to receive the commercial documents, it creates a "trade" acceptance. Because this acceptance is a negotiable financial instrument, it provides the seller and buyer with protection against risk found in other payment procedures, like open account; however, the risk of nonpayment increases significantly when using D/As. After exchanging an acceptance for the commercial documents, the buyer is in possession of the merchandise, whereas the seller has only the buyer's promise to pay at a later date. The presenting bank has no coercion over the buyer to pay by the acceptance's due date. Unlike a banker's acceptance, a trade acceptance (both of which are covered in "C. Drafts and Acceptances" in the Appendix) has only the credit backing of the buyer.

Rules/Documentation Needed

The two types of documents involved in the collection process are financial documents and commercial documents. Financial documents are instruments such as bills of exchange (drafts), payment receipts, or promissory notes. Commercial documents would include commercial invoices, bills of lading, shipping receipts, certificates of origin, or any other documents involved in the transit of merchandise. It is important to mention that collection procedures that involve both types of documents are known as documentary collections. Collections that involve only financial documents are considered "clean" documentary collections. Furthermore, collections involving parties abroad or banks in foreign countries are called foreign collections.

Documentary Collection Flow Chart

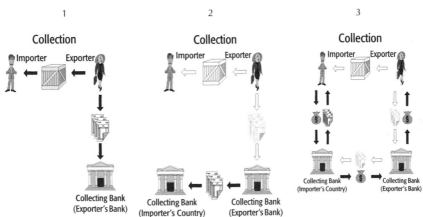

CHAPTER 4

CREDIT INSURANCE

Types of Insurance

There are three types of risks that need to be addressed in international trade: physical, commercial, and political. Fortunately, insurance exists to protect the seller/exporter against these risks. Insurance policies are grouped into three categories: Marine Cargo, Credit, and Country (Political) Risk policies.

Marine Cargo Insurance

A vital part of international trade transactions is protecting the shipment of merchandise against physical loss or damage during transit. This requires insuring the goods against shipment risks.

Whether or not the buyer or seller is required to purchase insurance for shipped merchandise depends upon the type of transaction specified in the export contract or purchase order. For example, if the seller is contracted to deliver merchandise to the buyer CIF (Cost, Insurance, and Freight), then the buyer/importer is responsible to insure the goods against risks while in transit to the destination specified. Carrier and shipping firms provide only minimal insurance for cargo they are instructed to deliver unless additional coverage is purchased.

Seeking insurance for physical damage to merchandise is a straightforward process that many commercial insurance firms and freight forwarders will provide. Sources of insurance are listed in the sections to follow. Regular exporters frequently use their own *open cargo* policy, which usually provides coverage from "warehouse to warehouse." This provides automatic coverage for the merchandise throughout the shipping process all the way to the customer's premises, thus minimizing any question as to where in transit a loss might have occurred. Policies for one-time shipments may also be available. However, for infrequent exporters, the best source of insurance, albeit perhaps more expensive, is the freight forwarder.

Insurance costs vary according to the extent of coverage, the risks specified, and any additional coverage requested by the purchaser. Typical coverage for a policy is 110 percent of the Cost, Insurance, and Freight (CIF) value. This extra 10 percent is a common level of coverage as it provides the insured party with modest compensation for the time and business lost while replacing a lost or damaged shipment.

How to Insure

Exporters shipping over $5,000,000 per year can usually save money by buying their own open policy, either through their regular insurance broker/agent, or from a specialty source. Others will find it more convenient and less expensive to use their freight forwarder's policy. Beware that forwarders surcharge their insurance cost to make this a profit center for themselves.

Terms and Conditions of Marine Cargo Policies

Marine cargo policies have been around since the 1700s; indeed the famous Lloyd's of London was founded to provide cargo insurance to British merchants. Many terms and conditions have not changed in 300 years, and a special branch of admiralty law has developed to address this unique market.

All Risk Coverage

By far the most common policy type in use today, this is a general coverage policy that is more expensive and more inclusive in its coverage, as it typically insures "against all risks of direct physical damage from an external cause" to the cargo. It is usually enhanced by the addition of Strikes, Riots, and Civil Commotion coverage and a separate, but complementary, war risk policy. Shippers of perishable commodities should be aware that standard "all risk" policies do not cover perils such as vermin, which are normally excluded as "inherent vice."

General Average Coverage

This type of policy provides compensation only in the event that part of a vessel's cargo is declared lost under general average by the carrier. For example, should a ship's captain need to dump cargo overboard to avert a disaster, declaring a loss under general average would spread the losses proportionally among all of those with cargo aboard, not just those whose cargo was sacrificed for the greater good. "Average" is an archaic old French term for loss—remember, this kind of insurance has been around for centuries!

Free of Particular Average (FPA)

Free of Particular Average refers to coverage where partial losses to a cargo are only covered under specific circumstances, such as the vessel being stranded, sinking, burning, and so on. This insuring term is often used for used equipment or machinery, where partial losses are hard to evaluate.

Strikes, Riots, and Civil Commotion (SR&CC) Coverage

This is typically endorsed to an all risk policy to cover the named risks, which are otherwise excluded.

War Risk Coverage

This policy coverage is usually issued in conjunction with other policies, either all risk or one of the average types. Because insurers often have separate protection for their own exposure to such risks, this is often written as a separate policy. Most insurance companies will not issue this type of policy for shipments to areas where there are imminent hostilities, and rates can fluctuate sharply.

Contingency Insurance

Regardless of the shipping terms and the fact that title to the goods may have passed to the buyer, there are still other, less assessable risks that the exporter may face, even with the appropriate marine insurance risks covered. These usually relate to the buyer's coverage on a FOB or similar shipment. In these cases, there is no way for the seller to know if the buyer insured the shipment at all.

If the buyer didn't, the consequences could be grave; however, even if the buyer did insure the cargo, how complete is the coverage? How reliable and financially sound are the policy and the insurance company? In what currency will the claim be paid? And can the foreign insurer transfer funds out of its own country to pay the claim with reasonable promptness? Even though the policy may be assignable, is it only payable in the buyer's country?

These issues can be solved by means of contingency insurance. It costs a fraction of regular insurance and is designed to protect a seller in a situation in which it reasonably relied on the buyer to insure the merchandise but sustained a loss because of inadequate coverage from the buyer. The contingency insurance will cover situations in which the FOB sales endorsement would have otherwise served had that been in force. Nevertheless, it may not be necessary to take this insurance in all situations. This will depend on the seller's knowledge, the insurance of the buyer, and how critical a potential loss might be.

Contingency coverage is usually added by endorsement to a shipper's open cargo policy.

Credit and Political Risk

These forms of insurance cover the exporter against the buyer's defaulting on its payment obligation (commercial risk) and/or its inability to pay owing to foreign government intervention, war, and so on (political risk). Both of these risks can be covered under "export credit insurance" policies. Sellers have the option of seeking only buyer credit risk insurance, only political risk coverage, or a combination of both, depending on their need.

Export credit insurance is used for a variety of reasons: to protect against the risk that the buyer won't pay invoices or against government intervention prohibiting the payment of foreign invoices; to encourage the extension of competitive credit terms to meet market demand; to secure accounts receivable for financing; to provide structure and discipline for export credit decision making; to gain leverage over potential problem accounts (credit underwriters have clout and resources well beyond most exporters); to finance overseas customers; to save time and money by replacing LCs with open account terms; and to enhance customer relationships (open account terms signify trust in a buyer's willingness and ability to pay). To determine the type of export credit insurance to obtain, if any at all, the exporter must follow the same prudent steps as it does domestically to ascertain the buyer's "credit standing" and payment history.

Short-Term Credit Insurance

"Short term" refers to sales on credit terms less than 360 days (typically 60 days or less) Most exporters need to be paid as quickly as possible, and do not want to grant longer terms than is absolutely necessary. Short-term policies can cover any type of good or service, including capital equipment.

- Why use short-term credit insurance?
  o Grant terms to match competition
  o Cheaper than LCs
  o Gives buyer time to receive and install or resell product before paying
  o Protects seller against default for political and commercial risks
- Features of short-term credit insurance
  o Either single sale *or* portfolio basis
  o Cost generally ranges between 0.25 percent and 1 percent of invoice ($250–$1,000 per $100,000)
  o Pay-as-you-go format or up-front deposit with adjustments based on sales

o Typical coverage is for 90–95% of loss, often after exhaustion of an aggregate deductible.

- Single sale vs. portfolio
  o Underwriters prefer a spread of risk. Single-sale approach means underwriters ask questions such as "Why are you buying insurance?" and "What is wrong with this deal?" since by definition the exporter is not insuring its other, presumably desirable, shipments.
  o Portfolio approach, insuring all shipments or a broad subsegment, means your good customers offset the not-so-good ones. Underwriters offer better terms on this basis than for single sales.
  o Many underwriters do not offer single-sale coverage due to perceived riskiness. Those who do charge steep minimum premiums and are very selective of the buyers they underwrite.
- Short-term creditworthiness
  o Underwriters may approve buyers automatically in many circumstances, based on seller's credit file and/or payment history, under a portfolio policy.
  o Larger credits, and all single-sale risks, are approved based on review of credit reports, financial statements, references, and so forth.
- Who provides short-term credit insurance?
  o Short-term insurance is available from a number of sources. Some examples of government and commercial insurers are:
    - Government: Ex-Im Bank
    - Commercial: American International Group, Inc., Atradius, HCC Credit, Coface, Euler Hermes ACI, Exporters Insurance Company, FCIA Management Company, and Lloyd's of London

Some insurers have their own sales forces selling their products exclusively; all will work with licensed and credentialed brokers. Many property-casualty brokers offer credit insurance to their customers, but most coverage is bought through independent specialists whose expertise is generally available at no additional cost to the exporter.

Buyer Credit Risk Analysis

Accurate and up-to-date credit information is even more important in international trade than in domestic transactions, because distances are longer and legal and business practices differ in most other countries. The prime tools for credit decisions and information on overseas customers are identical to those for domestic customers. Your own ledger experience remains one of the best sources if you have a history with the client. A valuable source that is commonly requested for domestic purposes, but often wrongly neglected in foreign business, is a financial statement from the buyer, especially if a large sum is at stake. Accounting is a universal language, although standard practices tend to vary between countries. In many transactions where export credit insurance is requested, a financial statement on the buyer is often required. Therefore, it should be every exporter's standard practice to obtain up-to-date financial information on each buyer.

Credit reports are also very important tools in the credit evaluation process. Even though your sales terms might stipulate LCs, without excellent credit your buyer might be forced to delay confirmation of orders until it becomes financially possible to open LCs. You might also have to make an investment relating to the shipment (raw materials, working capital) before the LC is received, so you would certainly want to know the credit standing of that client prior to the issuance of the LC. Another good reason to get a credit report is to have some assurance of the integrity of the client in case there is a discrepancy when collecting against LCs, because acceptance of noncritical discrepancies without delay is often a function of a business's operations and ability to pay. Another important reason for background information on your client, apart from its ability to pay, is knowledge and skill relative to the product being purchased and ability to competently conclude the transactions. Dealing with an unknowing or naive buyer is often the first step toward contract disputes, unjustified claims, or delays in payments.

Credit reports must be obtained as a precondition to obtain insurance from Ex-Im Bank, other export credit agencies, and many of the commercial insurers. Because it can take some time to get a completed report, it is always a good idea to request them well in advance of finalizing a contract or as soon as you feel there is a real possibility that you will be doing business with a particular overseas company.

Sources of Export Credit Information

Government Sources

The Department of Commerce offers its World Traders Data Reports (WTDRs), available through its district offices around the country. These reports are prepared by U.S. commercial officers in U.S. embassies abroad. They contain information on a company's business activities, its standing in the local business community, creditworthiness, its overall reliability and suitability as a trade contact, and the number of employees, ownership, products, and general operations. The WTDR is not specific as to trade references, amounts owing or overdue, or similar information you would expect to see in a domestic credit report. The Department of Commerce has special forms that need to be completed and returned with advance payment for each report to be processed. The cost varies but is usually $100–$150 per report. Allow six–eight weeks for processing in most countries. The WTDRs are one of the credit reports accepted by Ex-Im Bank.

Often, foreign buyers are well known to agencies like the Ex-Im Bank or to insurers. If you believe your buyer may have been covered previously by an insurer, request this information from the respective insurance company. This may save time, because Ex-Im Bank and other insurers each maintain files on foreign buyers whose credit they have checked as well as their experience with specific buyers. If recent information is already available, you may not need to request a new credit report. However, Ex-Im Bank will not share the information with you; they will only use it to evaluate a specific request.

United States embassies abroad can also be useful sources of country information through their economic attachés. These offices regularly report on the local economy as well as generating industry studies that include analyses of local corporations.

Domestic Sources

Dun & Bradstreet (D&B). The largest and best-known U.S. credit reporting and collection service agency, D&B's international division provides credit reports for its members on many foreign companies, although sometimes the information is dated. Reports can be ordered from their website at www.dnb.com. The D&B *World Marketing Directory of Principal International Businesses* may be available at a local library. This guide will provide some initial rating information.

FCIB-NACM Corporation. This is a trade association for executives in finance, credit, and international business, located at Koll Corporate Plaza, 485-A, Route 1 South, Suite 100, Iselin, NJ 08830-8613. Tel: (732) 283-8606, Fax: (732) 283-8613, and Internet: www.fcibglobal.com/. Its *International Special Credit Report Service* is compiled from a network of independent correspondents worldwide and provides very specific information about the company and the country in question. You must be a member of the association to access the service. Usage fees for service vary according to the country and type of report. The FCIB-NACM Corporation has excellent regional roundtable meetings for its members to discuss credit and collection experience on a country-specific basis.

Coface Services North America, Inc. Coface Services, based in New Haven, Connecticut, is the U.S. contact for the CreditAlliance network of credit reporting agencies. Coface sells credit reports worldwide, along with ratings and other services, from www.coface-usa.com. Reports are available singly or under a bulk contract.

Commercial Banks. Many banks offer credit-checking through their foreign correspondent banks or branch offices abroad. Some banks charge for these reports; others do not. Over the years, correspondent banks have become more reluctant to divulge meaningful information about their clients, owing to misinterpretations of the reports that in some cases led to lawsuits. At best, expect very sketchy information. The importance of bank-checking is really to determine that a banking relationship does, in fact, exist. To placate sellers, buyers will sometimes provide improper or wrong information. It is always better to be safe than sorry.

Foreign Sources

There are other sources of credit information serving many countries. They include: Auskunftei Buergel, P.O. Box 310, 5109 Aachen, Germany; Creditreform, P.O. Box 533, 4040 Neuss, Germany; and Asia Mercantile, throughout Asia.

 The Exporter's Guide to Foreign Sources for Credit Information lists details of credit firms in 45 countries and is a very good reference book. It can be obtained from Trade Data Reports, 6 West 37th St., New York, NY 10018.

 The Export-Import Bank of the United States publishes a list of credit reporting agencies that is available at www.exim.gov. Beware that this list was last updated in 2001.

Sources of Insurance for Commercial and Political Risk

Export-Import Bank of the United States

The Export-Import Bank of the United States (Ex-Im Bank) is an independent U.S. government agency chartered by Congress to facilitate the financing of exports of nonmilitary U.S. goods and services. By neutralizing the effects of export credit subsidies from other governments and by absorbing credit risks that the private sector will not accept, Ex-Im Bank enables U.S. firms to compete in overseas markets on the basis of price, performance, delivery, and service.

Ex-Im Bank's credit insurance policies provide protection against both the political and commercial risks of a foreign buyer defaulting on a credit obligation. Policies are available for single or repetitive export sales and for leases.

Small Exporters Getting Help

The Export-Import Bank of the United States, known as Ex-Im Bank, is responsible for financing and promoting U.S. exports. In the recent past, however, it has been assailed for neglecting small exporters. As an answer to its critics, Ex-Im Bank is now taking steps to increase loans and other services to smaller enterprises.

One example of the government agency's improvements is the loosened collateral requirement it now has for its working capital loan guarantee program. Companies use this program to borrow money for building export-related inventory and buying raw materials. Previously, collateral was measured mainly through the value of inventory. Now companies may include costs such as engineering, design, other overhead expenses, and export-related receivables in the collateral base, allowing for a greater amount of borrowing. Smaller companies with limited financial resources will especially benefit from this change, according to an Ex-Im Bank director. The working capital program is a strong example of the agency's commitment to smaller exporters. In the 2003 fiscal year, the program guaranteed 390 loans worth $768 million. This compares with 155 loans worth $180 million in fiscal year 1994. Much of the increase came from small companies' transactions, which account for 88 percent of the agency's deals and nearly 80 percent of its dollar volume.[4]

One small business that has benefited from Ex-Im Bank's working capital program is Cornet Technology Incorporated (CTI), a company specializing in high-speed communication products to customers in countries including Mexico, Brazil, Colombia, Surinam, Egypt, and South Korea.[5] Like many other small businesses, CTI was concerned about its ability to maintain cash flows needed to fill orders before

---

[4] Export-Import Bank of the United States, Annual Report 2003, www.exim.gov, accessed December 2004.

[5] Ken Murphy, "Cornet Technology Featured as Small Business Success Story in Export-Import Bank Annual Report," January 2004, www.exim.gov, accessed December 2004.

collecting customers' payments. Ex-Im Bank's working capital guarantee allowed the company to obtain commercial bank financing so that assets earmarked for export could also be used as collateral to obtain necessary funds. With the backing of Ex-Im Bank, CTI's president asserted that the company was "better equipped to export technologically advanced products to help increase productivity in every region of the world."

Even programs originally intended for large corporations are now widely used by small exporters. One example is the tied-aid program, which matches low-rate financing offered to foreign companies by their governments. Initially expected to benefit primarily large companies, about one-half of the tied-aid offers made by Ex-Im Bank now support small companies. For example, U.S.-China Industrial Exchange, Inc., a small Maryland exporter, received a tied-aid loan to sell more than $8 million in medical equipment to China.[6] A competitor, armed with tied-aid from the Austrian government, almost won the contract. "Unless we were also able to provide some favorable term-financing, we would have lost the business," said the company's president.

Small companies are increasingly making use of the agency's other programs, including credit insurance that protects American exporters and their banks against nonpayment from overseas buyers. In the last fiscal year, Ex-Im Bank authorized $1.4 billion in such insurance to nearly 2,000 small companies. The agency will continue to look for ways to attract small business customers, less so to deflect criticism but rather to support the growing number of small U.S. companies that are exporting and supporting jobs.

Ex-Im Bank offers short- and medium-term insurance policies to support export sales. The Small Business Policy is designed for U.S. firms with exports averaging less than $5 million over the preceding two years; and the Small Business Environmental Policy is for firms exporting environmentally related goods and services. Ex-Im Bank also offers short-term, single- and multibuyer policies, medium-term, single-buyer policies, and dealer plan

---

[6] Andrew Beadle, "The Export-Import Bank is a Resource for U.S. companies," *Journal of Commerce*, 8 March 2004.

coverage, which includes comprehensive medium-term coverage. Ex-Im Bank's insurance policies generally cover 100 percent of the principal for political risks and 90 percent to 95 percent for commercial risks as well as a specified amount of interest.

Short-term policies are used to support the sale of consumer goods, raw materials, and spare parts on terms of up to 180 days and bulk agricultural commodities, consumer durables, and capital goods on terms of up to 360 days. Capital goods may be insured for up to five years, depending upon the contract value, under medium-term policies. Exporters may obtain receivables financing more easily, because the proceeds of the policy are assignable to banks.

The Small Business Policy covers the repayment risks on short-term export sales by U.S. companies that have had a relatively small volume of exports over the previous two years, and that are considered "small" businesses under the Small Business Administration guidelines. The policy insures 100 percent of specified political risks and 95 percent of all other risks that might lead to default by the buyer, subject to policy conditions. Postmaturity interest, if any, is covered at a specified rate up to a limited time after the due date. The exporter must agree to include in the policy all its eligible sales. This policy insures short-term credit sales of goods and services. Premium is payable monthly in arrears, based on actual shipments made on credit terms. The premium rate varies by type of customer (government or private sector) and by credit terms. For example, open account terms up to 60 days to a private sector buyer cost 0.65 percent of the invoice amount, or $65 for every $10,000 sold on credit. Exporters can assign the rights to the amounts payable to a financial institution as collateral for obtaining financing.

The Short-Term, Single-Buyer Policy is custom written for a specified sales contract. Because the policy is structured for single-sale transactions, the standard period during which shipments can be made is three months. Ex-Im Bank can issue a policy for up to 12 months to accommodate multiple shipments under a sales contract. Under the policy, there is no requirement to insure a spread of business, thus allowing exporters to selectively insure transactions with or without linking them to bank financing. Coverage applies to credit sales to a specified foreign buyer for U.S. goods produced and shipped from the United States during the policy period. Cover is provided for credit terms up to 180 days. On a case-by-case basis, agricultural commodities, capital equipment, and quasi-capital equipment may be insured on terms up to 360 days. Percentages of cover are equalized for commercial and political risks: for sovereign obligors, 100 percent; private-sector and other nonsovereign obligors, 90 percent; LC transactions, 95 percent; bulk agricultural transactions, 98 percent.

The Short-Term, Multibuyer Policy is similar to the Small Business Policy described previously. It covers all eligible shipments made on credit terms during a one-year period. It provides coverage at lower premiums, helps the exporter to make quicker credit decisions (providing faster service to international buyers), and reduces paperwork compared to the Small Business version. The exporter can obtain financing and can offer competitive credit terms to attract and retain buyers around the globe, even in higher-risk markets. Premium rates are based on an exporter's credit term and country risk exposures and the policy has an annual aggregate deductible in addition to a 5 percent uninsured retention on each shipment.

The Medium-Term Policy covers individual or repetitive shipments to a single buyer of U.S. capital goods and related services sold on terms of up to seven years. These policies are usually sold to commercial banks or other financial institutions, and they allow foreign customers to finance their purchases at highly competitive interest rates normally not available in their country. Policies are written on a case-by-case basis and the exporter is not required to insure all medium-term transactions. The foreign buyer must make a 15 percent cash downpayment prior to shipment. The remaining financed portion is covered by a promissory note requiring payment in approximately equal installments generally on a semiannual basis. The policy covers interest charges up to specified limits as well as principal due. Coverage is 100 percent of a political and commercial loss.

Private Export Funding Corporation (PEFCO)

The Private Export Funding Corporation (PEFCO) is a consortium of private lenders that acts as a supplemental lender to traditional export financing sources. There are two distinct programs offered by PEFCO to support U.S. exports: Project and Product Buyer Credits, and Note Purchaser Facilities. The PEFCO loans, or purchased foreign importer notes, must be covered by the comprehensive guarantee of repayment of principal and interest by Ex-Im Bank. The Private Export Funding Corporation lends funds to foreign buyers of capital equipment or expensive products where the amounts are larger and/or repayment periods are longer than traditional lenders make for their own account. To be eligible:

- Ex-Im Bank Comprehensive Guarantee must be available
- Amount must exceed $1 million

- Fixed interest rate is required
- Final maturity must be over five years
- Any local or withholding taxes must be paid
- The loan request must come through a commercial bank

The PEFCO loans have ranged from $1 million to $225 million (with 5- to 22-year terms) and may be sponsored by domestic and foreign banks. Occasionally, PEFCO loans are made to commercial or special-purpose lessors or "borrowers of convenience," with the actual users of the equipment being obligors of the intermediaries. Terms and conditions reflect market conditions and are generally responsive to requirements of borrowers.

The Note Purchase Facility (NPF) was designed to provide assured liquidity to traditional lenders who use the Ex-Im Bank medium-term program. Under this facility, PEFCO will purchase from lenders or note-holders, or prospective lenders, with the Ex-Im Bank Guaranteed notes being used to finance U.S. goods and services. Eligibility requirements include:

- Security—Ex-Im Bank comprehensive guarantee
- Amount—Not in excess of $10 million
- Repayment—Seven years or less
- Interest Rate—Either fixed or floating with Ex-Im Bank guarantee on same basis
- Prepayment—Requires note-holder's consent

The PEFCO offers are based on current market conditions and purchase is without recourse to seller. Offers on existing notes carrying fixed or floating interest rates are available for up to two days pending response. Offers for pending commercial transactions may be made available to commercial banks on fixed- or floating-rate terms for extended periods at an additional cost. To settle an offer, PEFCO requires possession of the Note and an Ex-Im Bank Guarantee Agreement.

Department of Agriculture

Export Enhancement Program

The Export Enhancement Program (EEP) offers assistance designed to challenge unfair trading practices and encourage negotiation on agricultural trade problems, expand U.S. market opportunities for certain commodities to targeted destinations, and provide commodities to exporters as bonuses to make U.S. commodities more competitive in global markets by meeting competition from subsidizing countries. Since EEP's establishment in 1985,

112 initiatives have been announced with 75 countries. Sales pertaining to these initiatives have totaled more than $11.5 billion.

Eligible exporters are those that have at least three years' experience in exporting an eligible commodity. The company must also have an office and agent in the United States, provide evidence of financial responsibility, and provide various financial securities in connection with participation.

Credit Guarantee

Programs (GSM-102 and GSM-103) of the Commodity Credit Corporation (CCC) are designed to expand U.S. agricultural exports by stimulating U.S. bank financing to foreign purchasers. Financing through these programs is available in cases where credit is necessary to increase or maintain U.S. exports to a foreign market and where private financial institutions would be unwilling to provide financing without CCC guarantees.

The CCC covers the risk that a foreign bank might fail to pay under an LC for any reason. Failure to pay could result from circumstances ranging from the issuing bank's bankruptcy to foreign exchange controls imposed by the host government. In any case, CCC requires that the foreign buyer's bank issue an irrevocable LC, in U.S. dollars, in favor of the exporter covering payment for the commodities. Payment of interest to the U.S. bank that finances the transaction can be covered either by the LC or by a separate loan agreement between the U.S. bank and the foreign buyer's bank. These guarantees cover 98 percent of the principal and a portion of the interest on loans extended by guaranteed U.S. banks. No coverage is available for ocean freight under the guarantee.

The Export Credit Guarantee Program (GSM-102) provides the exporter or the exporter's assignee with the guaranteed repayment of six-month–three-year loans made to banks in eligible countries where U.S. farm products are purchased. Most major agricultural commodities are covered. The Intermediate Credit Guarantee Program (GSM-103), similar to the GSM-102 program, provides guarantees for 3- to 10-year loans.

Eligibility.   Commodities are reviewed on a case-by-case basis to determine eligibility. Particular requirements include operations in countries where such guarantees are necessary to secure financing and where there is enough foreign exchange to make the scheduled payments.

Rates.   The rate of interest is generally slightly above the prime lending rate or the London Inter-Bank Offered Rate (LIBOR).

The Commercial Export Credit Guarantee Agricultural Export Supplier Credit Guarantee Program

The Supplier Credit Guarantee Program (SCGP) administers export credit guarantee programs for commercial financing of U.S. agricultural exports. These programs encourage exports of U.S. agricultural goods to countries where importers can issue dollar-denominated promissory notes in favor of the U.S. exporters. Compared with the GSM-102 coverage, SCGP guarantees a substantially smaller amount of the value of exports (currently 65 percent) and does not cover interest.

Eligibility. Exporters who have previously qualified for GSM-102 or GSM-103 guarantees are automatically eligible for SCGP coverage. Other exporters must receive CCC qualification prior to accepting guarantee applications.

Contact:
CCC Operations Division
FAS/USDA
14th Street and Independence Avenue, SW
Washington DC 20250-1000
Tel: (202) 720-6211
Fax: (202) 720-0938
Internet Address: www.fas.usda.gov/excredits/scgp.html

Department of Defense

Defense Export Loan Guarantee (DELG) Program

The Defense Export Loan Guarantee (DELG) Program enables the Secretary of Defense to guarantee private-sector loans made to foreign sovereigns for the purchase or long-term lease of U.S. defense articles and services. The program strives to meet U.S. security objectives by encouraging interoperability of defense systems with its allies and to enable U.S. exporters to better compete in the international marketplace. The DELG program serves as a credit enhancement facility, allowing eligible foreign countries to achieve favorable borrowing terms and additional cash flow management flexibility.

The DELG program guarantees 85 percent of contract value or 100 percent of U.S. content, whichever is lesser in value. Defense exports must have a minimum of 50 percent U.S. content. The program offers a disbursement period (interest payments only) for up to 5 years and a repayment period up to 12 years. A cash payment of at least 15 percent of the contract value must be paid to the supplier prior to the disbursement of the guaranteed loan amount or in installments of at least 15 percent of the value of each payment.

The DELG program is similar to Ex-Im Bank's loan guarantee programs, except that foreign sovereigns bear all program costs, the exposure fee may not be included in the guaranteed loan amount, and the program pertains to defense exports as defined by the Arms Export Control Act only.

Eligibility.   Countries eligible for DELG assistance include NATO members, major non-NATO allies, emerging democracies of Central Europe, and noncommunist members of Asian Pacific Economic Cooperation (APEC). Eligible export items are defined in the Arms Export Control Act (22 U.S.C. 2751) and described in the United States Munitions List (22 CFR, Chapter I, Part 121). Appropriate export licenses from the U.S. Department of State are required before the Department of Defense will issue a final loan guarantee (see Chapter 2, page 23). The DELG guarantees may be applied to both direct commercial sales as well as sales made through the United States Foreign Military Sales program.

Contact:
Defense Export Loan Guarantee Program
Office of the Deputy Undersecretary of Defense
The Pentagon—Room 3E1082
Washington DC 20301-3070
Tel: (703) 697-2685
Fax: (703) 695-5343
Internet address: www.acq.osd.mil/icp/delg/defexploan.html

U.S. Small Business Administration

Export Financing Programs

The Small Business Administration's (SBA's) Export Finance Program guarantees short- or long-term loans to help small businesses acquire the financing needed to increase their export sales. These programs are designed to assist small businesses requiring capital to expand their manufacturing capabilities for export to international markets as well as to meet their working capital needs. Loan proceeds, however, may not be used to establish operations overseas.

Export Working Capital Program (EWCP)

The SBA's Export Working Capital Program (EWCP) helps small businesses export their products and services through credit lines for the expansion of export business. Proceeds can be used to finance labor and materials needed for manufacturing, purchasing goods or services, or foreign accounts receivable. The unique advantages of the EWCP program are simplified procedures (shorter application and fewer required documents) and a quick turnaround (generally 10 days or less).

Applicants must qualify under SBA's size standards and meet the other eligibility criteria applicable to all SBA loans. In addition, an applicant must have been in business (not necessarily international business) for at least 12 months prior to filing an application. The business must be current on all payroll taxes and have a depository plan for the payment of future withholding taxes.

The SBA can guarantee up to 90 percent of the principal and interest of a loan or $1,500,000, whichever is less. Borrowers may also have other current SBA guaranties, as long as the SBA's total exposure does not exceed $1,500,000. If the borrower has also secured an international trade loan (detailed in this section), the combined limit on SBA's exposure may not exceed $1.5 million. For loans that exceed this amount, the exporter must solicit funding assistance from another source, such as the Ex-Im Bank.

The maturity of an EWCP loan is based on an applicant's business cycle but cannot exceed 36 months, including all extensions. Borrowers can reapply for a new credit line when their existing line of credit expires. A new credit line, however, may not be used to pay off an existing line of credit. Interest rates are set through negotiations between the applicant and the participating lender. For maturities of 12 months or less, SBA charges a nominal fee of 0.25 percent on the guaranteed portion of the loan. In addition, the normal fees permitted on all SBA loans may also be assessed on EWCP loans.

Collateral may include accounts receivable, inventories, assignments of contract proceeds, bank LCs, or appropriate personal guarantees. The only acceptable collateral are those located in the United States and its territories and possessions or other assets under the jurisdiction of U.S. courts.

Export Express

The SBA has developed a new program to make obtaining working capital easier for small businesses. Under the Export Express program, the SBA has eliminated much of the paperwork typically associated with other working capital applications. The SBA will guarantee up to $250,000 on Export Express loans. This program focuses on single transactions requiring financing of six months or less.

International Trade Loan Program

The International Trade Loan Program provides long-term, fixed-asset financing to help small businesses establish or expand international operations. Loans are made through lending institutions under SBA's Guaranteed Loan Program.

Applicants for this loan must establish one of the following:

- The loan proceeds will expand their existing export markets or develop new export markets significantly; or
- The applicant's sales and profitability are adversely affected by increased competition from foreign firms.

In either case, the applicant may be asked to provide detailed narratives as well as financial statements.

Under this program, SBA can guarantee up to $2 million, less the amount of other SBA guaranties under the regular lending programs. For the International Trade Loan, SBA can guaranty up to 85 percent of loans of $150,000 and less, and up to 75 percent of loans above $150,000. The maximum guaranteed amount is $1,250,000. Interest rates range from 2.25 to 2.75 percentage points above the prime rate, depending on the maturity of the loan.

Proceeds from the loan may be used for working capital or for facilities and equipment, which includes purchase of land or buildings. Similar to other SBA programs, loan proceeds may not be used to pay off other debts. Only collateral located in the United States, including its territories and possessions, is acceptable for a loan made under this program. The lender must take a first lien position (or first mortgage) on the items financed. Furthermore, SBA may require additional credit assurances, such as personal guarantees and subordinations.

Contact:

Any SBA District Office (Appendix C) or
U.S. Small Business Administration
Office of International Trade
409 3rd Street, SW, 8th Floor
Washington DC 20416
Tel: (202) 205-6720
Fax: (202) 205-7272
Small Business Answer Desk
(800) 8-ASK-SBA
Internet Address: www.sba.gov

The Overseas Private Investment Corporation (OPIC)

The Overseas Private Investment Corporation (OPIC) offers political risk insurance to U.S. investors, contractors, exporters, and financial institutions involved in international business in industrializing countries. Insurance is available for new ventures or expansions of existing enterprises and can cover equity investments, parent company and third party loans and loan guarantees, technical assistance agreements, cross-border leases, assigned inventory or equipment, as well as other forms of investment.

Traditional Insurance Programs

The Overseas Private Investment Corporation offers a number of insurance programs designed to encourage U.S. private investment in projects in developing countries by protecting the investment from political risk. Policies can cover up to 90 percent of investments in qualified projects in eligible countries against loss due to certain political occurrences, including the following:

- Inability to convert profits denominated in local currency into dollars or return on the original investment;
- Loss due to expropriation, nationalization, or confiscation by action of a foreign government;
- Loss due to political violence such as war, revolution, insurrection, or civil strife; and
- Loss of business income due to interruption of the business caused by political violence or expropriation.

Overseas Private Investment Corporation insurance is specifically available to:

- U.S. citizens;
- Corporations, partnerships, or other associations created under the laws of the United States, its states or territories, and beneficially owned by U.S. investors (that is, more than 50 percent of each class of its issued and outstanding stock is owned by U.S. citizens either directly or beneficially);
- Foreign corporations at least 95 percent owned by investors eligible under the previously mentioned criteria; and
- Other foreign entities that are 100 percent U.S.-owned.

Eligible Countries.   The Overseas Private Investment Corporation provides coverage for U.S. private-sector investments in over 140 developing countries. Potential investors are urged to contact OPIC directly for an up-to-date list of eligible countries.

Eligible Investments. The Overseas Private Investment Corporation insures investments in new and existing enterprises for a maximum term of 20 years. With the exception of principal and interest from loans and leases from financial institutions to unrelated third parties, OPIC covers up to 90 percent of an investment (OPIC's statutes require that investors bear the risk of loss of at least 10 percent), not to exceed $200 million per project. Furthermore, OPIC typically issues insurance commitments equal to 270 percent of the initial investment—90 percent representing the original investment and 180 percent to cover future earnings. In addition, OPIC reserves the right to limit its coverage for investments in countries where it has a high portfolio concentration as well as highly sensitive projects.

Other Criteria. Investors are required to supply data on a project's developmental effect on the host country, including information relating to its environmental impact, job creation, skills development, balance of payments effects, as well as taxes and host government revenues.

The Overseas Private Investment Corporation will not provide investment coverage to projects that may have a negative effect on U.S. domestic employment and balance of payments. Furthermore, OPIC's bilateral agreements with host country governments require that the host country government approve each project for the purposes of OPIC's investment insurance. As a result, insurance coverage will not be provided until OPIC receives an acceptable foreign government approval of the proposed investment.

Inconvertibility. Coverage assures that earnings, returns of capital, principal and interest payments, and other remittances, including payments under technical service agreements, can continue to be converted into U.S. dollars. The insured will be compensated by OPIC for host country currency restrictions, whether they are active (host country authorities deny access to foreign exchange through regulations) or passive (host country monetary authorities fail to act on an application for hard currency). In either case, OPIC will make payments in the U.S. dollar equivalent of the local currency amount at an exchange rate in effect before OPIC received the application for compensation. Inconvertibility coverage does not protect against currency devaluation.

Expropriation. Coverage protects against the nationalization, confiscation, or expropriation of an enterprise, including "creeping" expropriation (that is, host government actions that deprive the investor of fundamental rights in a project for at least six months). Expropriation coverage does not protect against losses due to lawful regulatory or revenue actions by host governments and actions provoked or instigated by the investor or foreign enterprise.

Political Violence.   Political violence coverage protects investors from property and income losses resulting from violence undertaken for political purposes. Actions of political violence covered by OPIC include declared or undeclared war, hostile actions by national or international forces, civil war, revolution, insurrection, and civil strife, including politically motivated terrorism and sabotage.

Business Income and Damage to Tangible Property Coverage.   The Overseas Private Investment Corporation compensates for two types of losses: business income losses (losses of income resulting from damage to insured property) and damage to tangible property. For business income losses, OPIC compensation is based on income that would have been realized but for the damage; OPIC compensation is paid until productive capacity can reasonably be restored, not to exceed one year. For damage to tangible property, OPIC's compensation is based on the investor's share of the adjusted cost (defined as the lesser of the original cost of the item, the fair market value at the time of loss, or the cost to repair the item) or its replacement cost.

Terms.   The OPIC insurance contracts require the annual insurance premium to be paid in advance. Premiums are computed for each type of coverage on the basis of a maximum insured amount chosen by the investor on a yearly basis. The insured amount represents the insurance actually in force during any contract year.

The difference between the current insured amount and maximum insured amount for each coverage is called the standby amount. The major portion of the premium is based on the current insured amount; a reduced premium rate applies to the standby amount.

Premiums.   The OPIC's insurance premiums for most equity and shareholder debt investments are based on a maximum insured amount (MIA), a current insured amount (CIA), and a standby amount. The MIA represents the maximum insurance available for the insured investment and future earnings under an OPIC insurance contract. The CIA represents the amount of insurance actually in force during any contract period and must at least equal the book value of the insured investment unless a lower coverage ceiling is elected. The difference between the CIA and MIA is the standby amount. Annual premiums, once established, are fixed for the life of the OPIC insurance contract. Annual insurance premium rates (per $100 of coverage) for manufacturing and services projects are provided in the following table.

Coverage	Current (%)	Standby (%)
Inconvertibility	0.30	0.25
Expropriation	0.60	0.25
Political Violence*		
Business Income	0.45	0.25
Assets	0.60	0.25

*Discounted rates may be available for combined business income and assets political violence coverage.

Rates for natural resource and hydrocarbon projects, or very large projects, may vary by more than one-third of the base rates. The OPIC insurance contracts (except for those covering institutional loans and certain service contracts) contain provisions that allow for an increase in the initial current coverage rate by up to 50 percent during the first 10 years of the contract period and an additional 50 percent during the second 10 years of the contract period.

Subway Restaurants in Russia[7]

In 1994, Americans Bill Davies and Stephen Brown formed a joint venture with a Russian colleague, Vadim Bordug, to open the first Subway sandwich shop in St. Petersburg. By spring of 1995, however, the joint venture had fallen apart.

The American side accused Bordug of attempting to take control of the restaurant and illegally transferring $70,000 from Subway's St. Petersburg account in International Moscow Bank to a bank in Ireland. The Americans also contended that when Brown returned to work from vacation, the restaurant's security guards assaulted him

---

[7] Eric Schwartz, "Ruling for U.S. Firm in Subway Spat," St. Petersburg Times, 3 October 2003, http://archive.sptimes.ru/archive/times/907/sb/s_10534.htm, accessed August 2005.

and he had to take refuge in a locked office. Brown added that he was threatened by Bordug, who allegedly told him to "go back to America if he valued his life."

What resulted was a four-year running legal battle between Bordug and his former partners. First, Davies and Brown took the case to the Stockholm International Arbitration Court, which ruled in favor of the Americans' side and called for Bordug to pay $1.2 million plus interest to his former partners. Bordug disputed the ruling vociferously and appealed to the Russian Supreme Court for issues of jurisdiction.

As one of St. Petersburg's longest-running and most-watched business confrontations, the case and its ruling were affirmed by the Russian court. Although that meant that the U.S. partners could go to the St. Petersburg City Court to get the decision enforced, it brought on additional legal and personal difficulties. In spite of the extra legal obstacles that the U.S. partners faced, Bordug simply repudiated the courts' verdicts and failed to pay for the damages.

Fortunately for the U.S. partners, however, they had purchased $2 million in political risk insurance coverage on the Subway project from the Overseas Private Investment Corporation (OPIC), a U.S. organization that provides financing and insurance for business ventures abroad. The insurance policy covered what Bordug failed to pay, and the U.S. partners were able to continue with its aspirations of entering the Russian market. Less than 60 days after OPIC's coverage of the failed St. Petersburg Subway project, the U.S. partners were full-steamed ahead in opening up sandwich shop operations in Moscow.

Special Insurance Programs

In addition to OPIC's standard insurance program, the agency offers several insurance programs tailored to meet the special needs of certain types of investments. Investors are urged to contact OPIC to receive additional information regarding OPIC's special insurance programs as well as their premiums.

Financial Institutions. The Overseas Private Investment Corporation's political risk insurance allows U.S. banks and other institutional investors to better manage their cross-border exposures by insuring a wide range of banking activities, including project loans made or arranged by banks, gold loans, commercial paper transactions or floating-rate notes purchased by eligible institutions, cross-boarder leases, debt-for-equity investments, and commodity price swaps. Under this program, currency inconvertibility coverage compensates lenders/institutional investors for defaults on scheduled payments that result from a deterioration in the ability to convert these payments from local currency to U.S. dollars or to transfer dollars out of the host country. Furthermore, OPIC compensates the insured in the event the borrower defaults on a scheduled payment as a result of an expropriation or outbreak of political violence. To qualify for coverage under this program, the loan must have an average life of at least three years and the borrower must be a private enterprise in a foreign country.

Leases. The Overseas Private Investment Corporation provides insurance that can cover both capital and operating cross-border leases. This insurance is available to U.S. investors leasing to private sector entities for three years or more on an average life basis. For both capital and operating leases, inconvertibility coverage compensates for lease payments that cannot be converted from local currency to U.S. dollars or cannot be transferred out of the host country. For expropriations or political violence, compensation based on the value of the leased assets (including installation and transportation costs) is paid if these actions directly cause a default on a lease payment. In addition, OPIC provides coverage against host government actions that prevent a lessor from enforcing its right to repossess, reexport, and deregister leased equipment.

Oil and Gas. To encourage petroleum exploration, development, and production in developing countries, OPIC provides enhanced political insurance coverage that better meet the needs of the oil and gas sector. The OPIC enhanced expropriation coverage compensates the investor for losses caused by material changes unilaterally imposed by a host government on project agreements, including abrogation, impairment, and repudiation or breach of concession agreements, production sharing agreements, service contracts, as well as other agreements between the U.S. company and the foreign government. Expropriation compensation is based on the value of the insured investment/asset; OPIC will not compensate for loss of reserves of any kind. In addition to the enhanced expropriation coverage, OPIC insures against cessation of operations lasting six months or more as a result of political violence; however, the investor has the right and OPIC may require the investor to repurchase from OPIC its insured interests in the project if, within five years, the political violence ceases and the insured can resume operations.

Natural Resources (Except Oil and Gas).   For exploration phase natural resource projects, OPIC insurance can not only insure against confiscation and political violence losses to tangible assets, but also insure against the unlawful withdrawal or breach of mineral exploration, development, and other vital rights by the host government. Coverage under this program extends to equity, parent company or institutional loans, owners' guaranties of loans (including completion guaranties), and leases of equipment to project companies, among others.

Contractors and Exporters.   The Overseas Private Investment Corporation's insurance coverage for contractors and exporters protects the U.S. company from wrongful calling of bid, performance, or advance payment guaranties and customs bonds; loss of physical assets and bank accounts due to host country confiscation or political violence, as well as inconvertibility of proceeds from the sale of equipment used at the site; and losses due to unresolved contractual disputes with the foreign buyer. This insurance can protect U.S. companies acting as contractors in international construction, sales, or service contracts, and exporters of heavy machinery and other goods. Coverage under this program is issued when the U.S. company has a contract with a foreign government buyer.

Contact:
Insurance Department
Overseas Private Investment Corporation
1100 New York Avenue, NW
Washington DC 20527
Tel: (202) 336-8400
Fax: (202) 408-5142
Internet Address: www.opic.gov

Multilateral Investment Guarantee Agency (MIGA)

The Multilateral Investment Guarantee Agency (MIGA) was formed by the World Bank to facilitate foreign investment in developing member countries and to complement the activities of national investment insurance programs, private insurance companies, and the International Finance Corporation (IFC). The Multilateral Investment Guarantee Agency offers long-term political risk insurance and provides advisory and consultative services.

The guarantee program of MIGA is designed to encourage the flow of foreign private investment to emerging markets by mitigating political risks associated with a project. The Multilateral Investment Guarantee Agency offers long-term political risk insurance to project sponsors (that is, equity coverage) for new investments in developing member countries. Beyond insurance protection, MIGA's participation in a project enhances confidence that the investor's rights will be respected, an advantage inherent in the Agency's status as a voluntary association of developing and developed countries.

The coverage described below may be purchased individually or in combination, but selection of the desired coverage must be made by an investor before MIGA issues its guarantee. The maximum amount of coverage that MIGA can retain for a single project is currently $50 million, although the amount of coverage mobilized can be considerably expanded through MIGA's collaboration with other insurers, such as co-insurance. Following are the types of coverage offered by MIGA:

- **Transfer restriction.** Protects against losses arising from an investor's inability to convert local currency into foreign exchange for transfer outside the host country. Currency devaluations, however, are not covered.
- **Expropriation.** Protects against loss of the insured investment as a result of acts by the host government that may reduce or eliminate ownership of, control over, or rights to the insured investment.
- **War and civil disturbance.** Protects against loss from damage to, or the destruction or disappearance of, tangible assets caused by politically motivated acts of war or civil disturbance in the host country, including revolution, insurrection, coups d'état, sabotage, and terrorism.
- **Breach of contract.** Protects equity losses arising from the host government's breach or repudiation of a contract with the investor.

Eligible Investments. Unlike OPIC, MIGA can insure new investments originating in any member country (not just the United States) and destined for any developing member country other than the country of origin. New investment contributions associated with the expansion, modernization, or financial restructuring of existing projects are also eligible, as are acquisitions that involve the privatization of state enterprises. Eligible forms of foreign investment include equity and equity-like investments such as shareholder loans and loan guaranties issued by equity holders, provided the loans have a term of at least three years. Loans to unrelated borrowers (that is, by a commercial bank) can also be insured, provided a shareholder investment in the project is insured concurrently.

Duration of Guarantee. The Multilateral Investment Guarantee Agency's standard term of coverage is 15 years. Coverage may, in extraordinary circumstances, be extended to 20 years if MIGA finds that the nature of the project justifies it.

Premium Rates. The Multilateral Investment Guarantee Agency has established a premium fee structure (see following tables) that provides the basis for determining the premium rates that will apply to a specific investment. The Agency's risk assessment focuses primarily on the risks associated with the individual project and coverage, taking into account general economic and political conditions in the host country. Accordingly, the base rates noted may be raised or lowered for a particular project, depending on the project's risk profile. The rates are defined in the tables in relation to the type of industry and coverage and are applied to the amount of investment currently at risk ("current") and the amount expected to be at risk in the future ("standby"). All rates are per $100 of coverage.

I.   Manufacturing/Services

Type of Guarantee	Current (%)	Standby (%)
Currency Transfer	0.50	0.25
Expropriation	0.60	0.30
War and Civil Disturbance	0.55	0.25
Breach of Contract	0.80	0.40

II.   Natural Resources (includes agribusiness and forestry projects involving land ownership or concessions, or other types of projects where large landholdings are involved)

Type of Guarantee	Current (%)	Standby (%)
Currency Transfer	0.50	0.25
Expropriation	0.90	0.45
War and Civil Disturbance	0.55	0.25
Breach of Contract	1.00	0.50

III. Infrastructure/Oil and Gas

Type of Guarantee	Current (%)	Standby (%)
Currency Transfer	0.50	0.25
Expropriation	1.25	0.50
War and Civil Disturbance	0.70	0.30
Breach of Contract	1.25	0.50

Availability of Coverage

In each risk category, MIGA may insure equity investments for up to 90 per-cent of the investment contribution, plus an additional 450 percent of the investment contribution to cover earnings attributable to the investment. In the case of loans and loan guaranties, MIGA may insure up to 90 percent of the principal, plus an additional 135 percent of the principal to cover inter-est that will accrue over the term of the loan. For technical assistance con-tracts and similar agreements, MIGA insures up to 90 percent of the total value of payments due under the insured agreement.

Contact:
Multilateral Investment Guarantee Agency
1800 G Street, N.W.
Washington DC 20433
Telephone: (202) 473-6168
Facsimile: (202) 522-2630
Internet Address: www.miga.org

Marine Cargo Insurers

Most commercial insurance companies trace their corporate roots to the marine cargo industry, and therefore continue to offer this product. Both specialty and generalist insurance brokers can help exporters obtain cover-age at competitive rates. Freight forwarders also offer exporters the use of their master policies, albeit at a profit to the forwarder.

Sources of Country Risk Information

In assessing your international risks, don't forget to consider country risk, regardless of the creditworthiness and reputation of the buyer. If there is a coup, war, strike, or lack of foreign exchange in the buyer's country, the buyer will probably not be able to pay, either temporarily or permanently.

Your only hope of payment may then be under the political risk portion of your export credit insurance policy. Obviously, there are many countries whose stability is apparent, but there are many more borderline cases than you might suspect and some where it is impossible to obtain any coverage. To recognize potential country risk, watch for political unrest, high interest rates and inflation, balance of trade, and balance of payments deficits.

There are a number of sources for determining country risk, including: The Department of Commerce, Ex-Im Bank, the Department of State, the CIA, FCIB-NACM, insurance companies, international departments of commercial banks, and freight forwarders. In addition, there are many private sources that specialize in providing country information, including:

- International Reports, IRM (USA) Inc., New York, NY
- S.J. Rundt & Associates, New York, NY
- Business International Corp., New York, NY
- The Chase World Guide for Exporters, New York, NY
- The Economic Intelligence Unit, Ltd., New York, NY
- Dun & Bradstreet, New York, NY
- Various publications: *Euromoney, The Economist, New York Times*

A truly valuable tool for any exporter in evaluating country risk is the *Country Limitation Schedule,* published by the Ex-Im Bank generally each May and November. This publication identifies those countries where Ex-Im Bank is doing business and those that are "off limits" or where activities are limited or restricted. Because Ex-Im Bank is required to find a "reasonable assurance of repayment" in every transaction it undertakes, its position in a country is often a good indicator of risk level.

CHAPTER 5

OPEN ACCOUNT

What Is It?

This payment procedure requires the seller to provide the merchandise to the buyer in return for payment at a later, predetermined date. The payment terms of open account transactions are usually stated as a certain number of days after the receipt of goods. Using this procedure, the buyer of goods and services has very little risk exposure, in contrast to the seller or manufacturer. The buyer can withhold payment to the seller if there is any question about the quality or quantity of the merchandise. The buyer also can inspect the merchandise prior to taking ownership, giving him/her the opportunity to address any problems. This "Right of Inspection" reduces the buyer's risk of paying for unsatisfactory merchandise, because the buyer can decline payment until satisfied with the merchandise.

By contrast, the seller undertakes considerable risk with open account transactions. The seller must provide merchandise acceptable to the buyer or risk payment default. Also, the seller must risk the possibility that the buyer will accept the merchandise and refuse to pay. Such circumstances dictate that the seller thoroughly investigate the creditworthiness and integrity of the buyer prior to making open account arrangements. The seller usually reserves the use of open account transactions for well-established customers with good credit ratings.

Generally, it is ill-advised to trade internationally on open account terms. Because there is no written evidence of debt in open account transactions other than perhaps a written purchase order and corresponding invoice, the exporter must put significant faith in the buyer. Worst of all, there is no guarantee of payment. If the debt turns bad, the problems of overseas litigation are considerable. Furthermore, in less-developed countries, many importers need proof of debt in applications to the central bank for hard currency. Therefore, open account terms are ideal only for multinational corporations settling internal transactions or when trade partners harbor implicit trust and business integrity, the buyer's credit and commercial history are exceptional, and means to redress any grievances in the buyer's home country exist and are available to the exporter. However, export credit insurance policies can protect the seller against default, and make open account terms a real possibility.

Telecom Woes in Latin America

In the mid-1990s, a major telecommunications company realized that it had ignored a potentially attractive market in Latin America. It decided to enter the market and hired a group of aggressive salesmen from numerous Latin American countries. Although the company was very conservative, it did not know the market well and decided it needed to penetrate the market quickly to establish itself. Faced with competition that had a head start in the region, the company allowed the salesmen to negotiate with flexible payment terms.

The company became successful very quickly. Why? The salesmen began selling in the most flexible way possible to gain sales. This meant that it began selling on open account. This worked very well in the initial years. Sales were growing nicely and ultimately exceeded $100 million a year in the region. The only problem with this strategy was that the company had difficulty collecting payments in a timely manner. Until 2000, this was never a major problem because the stock market was booming and the company had plenty of cash on hand, so it felt it could afford the delayed payments problems in this region.

This changed dramatically later that year when the stock market crashed. With a tumbling stock price and increased borrowing costs, this company needed as mush cash as it could get. Because of this sudden change in market conditions, the Latin America portfolio was now a major problem for this telecommunications company.

The company's only solution was to stop selling and to focus on collecting these open account receivables as quickly as possible. This became an annoyance to its customers. The company had a decision to make. Was it going to stop selling in the region and alienate its customers, or was it going to implement a different sales strategy? What to do? The company decided it was best if it could implement a Letter of Credit (LC) policy. This is not the logical way to do business with an existing customer base, but the company had to try something if it wanted to stay in the region.

What was the result? Most of the company's important customers began doing business on an LC basis, and the company slowly improved its cash-flow condition in Latin America.

What should the company have done to avoid this problem from the beginning? It should have studied its payment options more carefully and implemented an LC strategy, or used export credit insurance, instead of using open account terms just to get the business.

CHAPTER 6

CONSIGNMENT

Consignment selling allows the importer to defer payment until the goods are actually sold. Furthermore, titles to the goods remain with the exporter until all the purchase conditions are satisfied. This type of arrangement can be advantageous, as it may allow exporters to be commercially competitive and permit them to recover unsold goods.

Consignment arrangements, however, place the entire burden of ownership and payment risk on the exporter. Thus, its use should be carefully weighed against the objectives of the transaction. The arrangement will require clear understanding of the parties' responsibilities, especially details regarding who is accountable for insurance at different stages of the transaction.

One of the greatest disadvantages of consignment selling is recovering unsold goods from the foreign consignee, which can be costly and time-consuming. In particular, the exporter must clear the goods through customs by paying or avoid paying duties or try to get refunds on previously paid duties. Moreover, the seller must be well versed in local laws concerning transference of title and taxation.

Owing to the complex nature of international customs regulations, it may behoove the exporter in consignment arrangements to enlist the support of a customs broker. Customs brokers are responsible for preparing and filing necessary customs entries, arranging the payment of duties, taking steps to affect the release of the goods in customs custody, and representing clients in custody matters.[8] Contacts of a few international customs brokers follow:

Flegenheimer International, Incorporated
227 W. Grand Avenue
El Segundo, CA, 90245
Tel: (310) 322-4366
Fax: (310) 322-5206

---

[8] "The Role of Customs Brokers". U.S. International Trade Data System. U.S. Department of the Treasury. 23 April 2004. Accessed from http://www.itds.treas.gov/broker.html in July 2005.

K International Transport, Incorporated
74 Trinity Place, 20th Floor
New York, NY 10006
Tel: (212) 267-6400
Fax: (212) 267-6403

KCarlton International
P.O. Box 21671
Ft. Lauderdale, FL 33335
Tel: (954) 525-9707
Fax: (954) 525-9708

PART II

TERM FINANCING

CHAPTER 7

FORFAITING

The name *forfaiting* is derived from the French term for the technique *a forfait*. It refers to the concept that the seller forfeits the right to a future payment on a receivable in return for immediate cash. This may sound similar to factoring. The differences are that forfaiting usually covers very large single transactions for a term of between one and five years, whereas factoring generally involves a smaller continuous stream of receivables with maturities of one to six months. Forfaiting has been a major financing tool in Europe for decades. Only in recent years has the concept been available to U.S. companies. The key forfaiting houses continue to be dominated by European banks, most notably London Forfaiting through FIM Bank, HSBC Bank, and others. Most of these firms have offices in New York and in some other U.S. cities.

Forfaiting offers fixed-rate financing but usually only on capital goods and equipment, and there always must be an underlying transaction. It is nonrecourse financing to the exporter owing to nonpayment by the buyer/guarantor. The forfaitor, however, does retain recourse to the seller for product performance issues and document authenticity. Unlike factoring, the underlying debt instrument is usually a promissory note signed by the buyer and guaranteed by a reputable bank in the buyer's country. If the buyer is well known or is a government entity, the bank guarantee may not be required.

Forfaiting is attractive when the seller and buyer get together early in the contact process and consider financing options. Forfaitors quote an all-in financing rate for the transaction well before the merchandise has been sold. If the buyer agrees to the rate, then the interest rate is added into the cost of goods and included in the total invoice and promissory note values. In this manner, when the goods are shipped and valid documents presented to the factor, sellers receive 100 percent of their merchandise value in cash, as a discount from the total amount of the promissory note (which includes the factor's interest rate). When the note is paid in full, the forfaitor receives the money for the amount paid to the seller, plus its interest rate. An example of a forfait follows, with details of the transaction's steps:[9]

---

[9] "Example". Trade and Export Finance Online. http://www.tefo.org/products/forfait-financing.php. 2005. Accessed July 2005.

Select Homes

In 1999, two massive earthquakes hit northwestern Turkey, the country's most densely populated region and industrial heartland. Izmit, a city of one million and the location of the epicenter, experienced 18,000 casualties and damages to 300,000 homes and 40,000 business buildings.

Shortly after the quakes, Select Homes, a housing manufacturer in Sacramento, received a call. A cement company in Turkey had heard of Select and its housing technology, which revolutionized the way structures are built. Select produces insulating concrete forms that are hollow blocks that are staked into the shape of a building's exterior walls. After the forms are fastened with adhesives, reinforced concrete is poured inside. The end result is a foam-concrete sandwich that is water- and termite-proof and wind- and earthquake-resistant. Select ultimately sold a license agreement to the Turkish cement company, which became a joint-venture partner.

Together, the joint venture received a contract from the Turkish Housing Ministry for 52 schools. The joint venture purchased a manufacuring facility from Select Homes for $649,000. The joint venture could not qualify for three-year financing on its own but was able to get a Turkish Development Bank guarantee. Select found a London Forfait House willing to finance the transaction through forfait trade financing. The transaction took the following steps:

- The commercial contract was signed with the Turkish Housing Ministry.
- A forfaiting agreement was signed with the London Forfait House.
- The manufacturing facility was shipped and delivered.
- The promissory note drafts were delivered to the Forfait House.
- The drafts were endorsed according to forfaiting agreement along with shipping and trade documents, including the invoice.
- Select was paid the total amount of all drafts less discount.

- London Forfait House made presentation of drafts for collection at maturity to the joint venture.
- The joint venture made payment of all drafts as agreed.

As the example illustrates, forfaiting can be an attractive financing alternative to traditional bank sources. Although requiring a great deal of discipline and patience, it is used increasingly as a source for financing the 15 percent down-payment requirement under Ex-Im Bank transactions. Forfaiting is particularly useful in this transaction, because buyers normally do not have the 15 percent cash on hand. Additional benefits of forfaiting for the exporter are as follows:

- Exporter can offer credit to buyer but receive cash payment immediately upon delivery of the goods or services.
- There are no country-of-origin restrictions as required by Export Credit Agencies.
- Up to 100 percent of sale can be financed at "nonresource" terms.
- Forfaiting also
  o Eliminates the two key risks—political and commercial credit risks
  o Improves competitive advantage by providing vendor financing
  o Eliminates export credit insurance premiums and commercial banking fees

Although forfait houses are an attractive outlet for financing this requirement, the problem with forfaiting is that it does not work for small transactions. Usually, transactions need to be above $500,000 and for terms of greater than one year to be of interest to the forfait market. Unfortunately, this financing alternative has limited application for small companies. Additional disadvantages are listed below:

- Forfait financing does not cover predelivery risks.
- An export shipment is effectively "open account" until a commitment is obtained from the forfaitor and the exporter fulfills its obligations.
- Exporter has the responsibility to ensure that the debt is legal, enforceable, and properly guaranteed.
- The cost of forfait financing can be higher than commercial bank financing.

Most major U.S. banks have contacts with the key factoring houses and can help customers access this financing technique. Regardless of the specific factoring house, generally required documents are a

- Copy of the sales contract;
- Copy of the signed commercial invoice;
- Copy of shipping documents such as bill of lading, evidencing delivery, and receipt of goods;
- Letter of assignment and notification to the guarantor; and
- Letter of guarantee, or the "aval."

Factoring

Factoring is defined as the purchasing of accounts receivable by a "factor." Although the use of factoring in international trade goes back centuries, the practical use of this financing option is relatively new to U.S. corporations.

Factoring is offered under an agreement between the factor and a seller. Under the agreement, the factor purchases the seller's accounts receivable, normally without recourse, and assumes the responsibility for the debtor's financial ability to pay. If the debtor goes bankrupt or is unable to pay its debts for credit reasons, the factor will pay the seller. Thus, the role of the factor is to collect money owed from abroad by approaching importers in their own country, in their own language, and in the locally accepted manner. As a result, distances and cultural differences can cease to be a problem.

Factoring has become well established in developing countries, particularly those that are highly industrialized. In various Asian countries, the growth of factoring has been dramatic, and in Latin America, financial institutions continue to join the industry. Similar growth has occurred in Central Europe, the Baltics, and the Middle East.

Like all other financing options, factoring has its pros and cons. One of its major appeals is that it provides exporters with an opportunity of getting cash from an export sale, particularly open account sales, without having to show a liability on their books in the form of a loan. This results because the factor usually purchases accounts receivable "without recourse" to the exporter. Therefore, factoring can be very attractive to young and rapidly growing small to medium size enterprises, because cash flow is preserved and risk is eliminated.

Arrangements between export and import factors can fall within a broad spectrum. On the one side is the traditional two-factor service, in which the export factor is heavily dependent upon the services of the import factor.

On the other end is the direct export service, whereby the export factor requires no or very little service from the import factor. In between the two are full factoring, collection only, nonnotified factoring, export bulk factoring, and fast cash factoring. These services, all of which can be tailored by factors to meet exporters' and importers' specific needs, are detailed below:[10]

- **Two-factor service** is applicable in situations where the export factor wants the import factor to be in full control of the combination of credit cover, dunning, and collection services in the importer's country.
- **Full factoring** is an agreement in which the factor is responsible for sales ledger accounting, credit cover up to 100 percent, and the collection of receivables.
- **Collection only** applies when the factor simply collects the receivables and maintains the sales ledger administration.
- **Non-notified factoring (NNF),** or confidential invoice discounting, occurs when the factor's main role is to provide credit protection in a confidential environment. That is, there is no notification of the assignment of the debt. Sales ledger administration remains under the client's control and payments are made directly to the export factor or exporter, and the import factor assumes responsibility for collection at a predetermined time after the due date.
- **Export bulk factoring** is pertinent when the factor provides services similar to an NNF arrangement but without the confidentiality (the debtor is immediately notified of assignment of the debt).
- **Fast cash factoring (FCF)** is applicable in situations when the export factor wants the import factor to provide credit cover and dunning services, while the debtor is advised to pay directly to the export factor in order to speed up the collection process.
- **Direct export factoring** is an agreement in which the export factor will control the credit cover, dunning, and collection process without the involvement of an import factor.

Another advantage of factors is the array of support services they provide, including complete credit research on foreign companies, credit decisions for the exporter, and advance funds for accounts receivable of up to 100 percent without recourse. Other firms may require the exporter to do

---

[10] "Export Factoring Options". International Factors Group. http://www.ifgroup.com/2005public/factoring-export.asp. 2005. Accessed July 2005.

the credit investigations and may advance smaller percentages of the accounts receivable with recourse to the seller. The cost of the service depends on the extent of assistance provided by the factor, volume of the exporter's business, its collection experience, the countries involved, and the average dollar size of the receivable portfolio. Cost will also depend on other variables, including the exporter's financial strength, experience, stability, the diversity (or spread) of portfolio risk, and the degree of concentration in higher-risk countries.

With the benefits of factoring services in mind, it is imperative to note its disadvantages. For U.S. companies, a potential problem is that factors do not cover a broad cross-section of countries, because most factors are "niche" players, who concentrate in select regions of the world. Furthermore, factoring service is usually cost prohibitive for smaller companies. If cost and security are issues, it is generally cheaper to use an LC or export credit insurance.

There are a number of well-known factoring companies. Among the largest are

- Factors Chain International
  Keizersgracht 559
  1017 DR Amsterdam
  The Netherlands
  Phone: +31-20-6270306
  Fax: +31-20-6257628
  E-mail: fci@fci.nl
- Heller Financial Incorporated
  500 West Monroe Street
  Chicago, IL 60661
  Phone: 312-441-6878
  Fax: 312-441-7367
- International Factors Group
  Avenue R. Vandendriessche, 18 (box 15)
  BE - 1150 Brussels
  Belgium
  Phone: +32/2/772-6969
  Fax: +32/2/772-6419
  E-mail: info@ifgroup.com

CHAPTER 8

MEDIUM-TERM LOANS

These are transactions financed for periods of between one and seven years and normally include only capital equipment. This is the principal area in which government programs operate, because commercial banks and finance companies are generally short-term lenders. Many of these transactions will require the guarantee or aval of a bank in the buyer's country. This is especially true if the buyer's financial condition is not good enough for the buyer to get the financing on its own. Medium-term financing is advantageous because buyers get up to five years to pay at interest rates much lower than those available in their respective countries. Also, the seller gets paid in full upon shipment. We will deal with the details of this type of financing when government programs are discussed in a later chapter.

How Does It Work?

Buyer pays seller a down payment.
Buyer signs promissory notes to Lender.
Lender pays seller balance upon shipment.
Buyer pays lender semiannual installments.
If Buyer defaults, lender has protection.

Medium-Term Requirements

Interest rates for medium-term loans generally range between the London Inter-Bank Offered Rate (LIBOR)-plus-one percent and LIBOR-plus-three percent and can be either fixed or floating. Rates are applied to 85 percent of the balance, and the resulting premium is eligible for financing.

Similar to other trade finance methods, medium-term financing often necessitates assistance from international finance specialists, especially in providing premium rate indications and identifying the most beneficial option. One such experienced company is *Interlink Capital Strategies,* a Washington DC-based international finance consulting firm managed by principals who have gained numerous years experience at the U.S. Ex-Im Bank and other export credit agencies. Its contact details are as follows:

Interlink Capital Strategies
7700 Leesburg Pike, Suite 201
Falls Church,VA 22043
Phone: 703-752-5880
Fax: 703-752-7999
E-mail: info@i-caps.com

Importance of Collateral and Security

Depending on the nature of a trade transaction and the seller's credit risk analysis and risk appetite, collateral and security may be important issues. Collateral is usually requested in a transaction when the buyer's ability to pay is in question. By providing collateral, buyers are offering sellers or financing entities a secondary source of payment in the event that the buyers are unable to make payments on their debt obligation. Collateral may be required in some cases even when a guarantee is being provided. The best collateral is that which can be readily sold or liquidated. This type of collateral is considered "liquid" or readily negotiable. It includes currency, stock and/or bond certificates, and negotiable instruments like bank certificates of deposit.

When capital equipment is being sold, often the seller or financing entity will want to take a security interest in the equipment that is being financed. In the event of a payment default by the buyer, the financing entity would be able to repossess the equipment. The ability to perfect a security interest in the equipment being financed is dependent on the laws and business practices in the buyer's country. In some cases, acquiring a security interest is fairly straightforward, and in other cases, it can be very difficult.

Recourse

Recourse is commonly referred to in the world of structured trade finance. It is the concept of retaining certain financial obligations in a transaction. When companies sell their goods or services they normally expect to receive payment in full. When they receive payment, they do not want that payment to be encumbered in any way. Sometimes financial institutions require the payment of funds to sellers to be made with recourse to the seller. This means that if the sellers have not completely fulfilled their contractual obligations to the buyer, they may be asked to return some of the funds already paid. This concept is always an issue with product performance and product quality. Most medium-term export transactions financed by governments require recourse to the seller for product-related disputes.

Nonrecourse

All exporters want to sell their goods and services on a nonrecourse basis. This means that once the sale has been completed and the payment has been made, no one can request the seller to return any portion of the payment. Most short-term transactions are handled on a nonrecourse basis. If buyers want to protect themselves on product-quality issues before paying for the product, then they can require an inspection of the product prior to shipment.

Extending Credit

Protection for medium-term financing is usually in the form of either credit insurance or a credit guarantee.

Medium-Term Credit Insurance

Single sales from $75,000 to $10 million
Repayment terms from one to five years
Underwritten mainly by the Ex-Im Bank, an independent federal agency
Four- to six-week approval process

Medium-Term Guarantees

Over $10 million per sale (can be lower)
Unconditional guarantee of payment, issued by Ex-Im Bank
Three- to four-month approval process
Slightly more expensive than similar insurance

Role of Guarantees and Avals

Guarantees

In many international transactions, after the financial analysis of the buyer is complete, it is determined that, for the transaction to be finalized, a guarantee is required. Normally a commercial bank guarantee is requested. Sometimes a government guarantee is necessary, depending on the nature of the transaction and the buyer's corporate status.

Avals

Similar to guarantees, avals are used in some countries instead of guarantees. Many Latin American countries use avals. Whether a guarantee or aval is used, the result is the same. If the buyers do not honor their payment obligations, then the guarantor will be required to make those payments. If an aval or guarantee is required in a transaction, the buyer's financial costs increase.

What Information Is Required to Show Creditworthiness?

Three years' financial statements, preferably audited, including notes, etc.
Favorable credit agency report
Two favorable supplier trade references
Favorable bank reference
Explanation of any material negative information

What Key Financial Ratio Is the Benchmark?

After purchase price is added to buyer's balance sheet, total liabilities should not exceed 40 percent of equity.

What If Buyer Is not Creditworthy?

Transfer payment risk to another party, such as a parent company or financial institution.
Personal guarantees of principal owners may be required.

Where Is Ex-Im Bank Coverage Available?

Ex-Im Bank is open in most countries.
Certain countries for political and commercial reasons are very difficult.
Contact *Interlink Capital Strategies* for latest information.

CHAPTER 9

GOVERNMENT

Export Credit Agencies (ECAs)

Historical Overview

Export credit agencies have been operating for over 70 years. The Ex-Im Bank was founded in the 1930s specifically to help finance grain sales to Russia. From that humble beginning, Ex-Im Bank has developed into numerous financing programs offered in over 120 countries. It, along with some of the European ECAs, has set the standard for the proliferation of these types of financing programs throughout the world. An excellent resource guide on the subject produced by the author is *Inside the World's Export Credit Agencies,* published by Thomson.

Export credit agencies have had the reputation of only catering to the needs of large corporations. Their programs were perceived as difficult to understand, involving a lot of patience and expertise that only large companies could afford. This perception has changed substantially during the past few years as more and more small and medium sized enterprises (SMEs) take advantage of the financing tools needed to succeed in emerging markets. Because small businesses represent 60 percent of all exporters in the United States (only 30 percent of exported goods and services), the U.S. government wants this percentage to grow! For small businesses to gain easier access to its programs, Ex-Im Bank set up regional offices around the country and has allowed the SBA to offer to its constituents some of Ex-Im Bank's programs.

Grow Jobs via Exports

All ECAs believe that domestic employment is created when companies export. Because every country would prefer a balance of trade surplus, most countries have set up ECAs to promote exports. In many cases, these agencies have become powerful agents of change and somewhat political. This is unfortunate but inevitable in a very competitive world.

The Export-Import Bank of the United States

Goal/Mission

The Export-Import Bank is an independent U.S. government agency chartered by Congress to facilitate the financing of exports of U.S. goods and services. Its principal goal is to increase U.S. jobs through exports. By neutralizing the effects of export credit subsidies from other governments and by absorbing credit risks the private sector will not accept, Ex-Im Bank enables U.S. firms to compete fairly in overseas markets on the basis of price, performance, delivery, and service.

Policies

In pursuing its objectives, Ex-Im Bank works within a set of policies that focus on creating U.S. jobs and adhering to U.S. laws and regulations. As a result, Ex-Im Bank has certain restrictions in using its programs, which may prevent some companies from getting its support.

What are these restrictions? To ensure that their programs are creating jobs domestically, Ex-Im Bank requires that at least 51% of the value of insured goods be of U.S. origin, and that all products must have final manufacturing stage in, and be shipped from the United States. Finally, with few exceptions, no product can be shipped to a military buyer. Within these restrictions, Ex-Im Bank can support a variety of trade transactions under numerous programs.

Pre-Export Programs

Working Capital Guarantee Program (WCGP)

This program gives U.S. exporters access to working capital loans from commercial financial institutions. By providing 90 percent repayment guarantees to lenders on secured short-term loans against inventory and foreign receivables, exporters obtain the necessary working capital to purchase inventory, build products, and extend terms to overseas buyers. This program provides the means for SMEs to pursue exports more aggressively. Working capital guarantees can be issued for specific transactions or for a series of transactions in the form of a line of credit.

Ex-Im Bank will issue its guarantee to the lender if, in its judgment, the eligible exporter is creditworthy for the loan or line of credit to be guaranteed. The creditworthiness of an exporter is determined by assessing financial information, management, track record, and the type of transaction to be financed. Before issuing a guarantee to a lender with which it has no working experience, Ex-Im Bank may require a full financial disclosure. The lender must be able to demonstrate the ability to service loans to exporters in accordance with Ex-Im Bank's guarantee. The lender must also certify that the loan would not otherwise be made without the guarantee. Exporters must be based in the United States, but ownership can belong to either a foreign national or entity. Start-up and developmental stage entities are ineligible.

The content of the product is also a major eligibility factor. If the cost of a product is made up of less than 50 percent U.S. content, then only the cost of the U.S. content may be eligible for financing. If the cost of a product is made up of at least 50 percent U.S. content, then the entire cost of that product may be eligible for financing, provided that the non-U.S. content portion is incorporated into the product in the United States.

The terms of a loan can be up to 12 months but may be longer if required in the case of a loan that supports a single export transaction (transaction-specific loan). For multiple export transactions (revolving loan), terms can be up to 36 months. The guarantee is for 90 percent of the principal amount of the loan and interest. Ex-Im Bank requires that the lender retain 10 percent risk in the loan, which cannot be collateralized separately. Additionally, the lender must be secured with inventory of exportable goods, accounts receivable on goods or services already exported, or other acceptable collateral.

Ex-Im Bank charges a $100 processing fee as well as a nonrefundable facility fee of 1.5 percent of the loan amount, payable within five business days of the loan closing date. For lower-risk transactions, as determined by certain Ex-Im Bank criteria, Ex-Im Bank charges only one percent of the loan amount.

Ex-Im Bank requires the following types of information for the requested loan guarantee:

- Information on the goods to be financed (for example, cash flow, terms of payment)
- A summary of the exporter's business plan and history of activities
- Three years of audited financial statements
- A recent interim financial statement, including aging of accounts receivable and payable
- At least five credit and/or bank references
- A summary of management's experience in related and nonrelated fields
- For newly formed trading companies or other exporters, an opening balance sheet may be submitted in lieu of this information

Application forms are available from Ex-Im Bank directly or online at its Internet site. From the information provided by the applicant, Ex-Im Bank will decide whether the request meets the program guidelines and offers a reasonable assurance of repayment. If the applicant is the lender, it is required to submit its own credit analysis and describe how it will control disbursement and application of funds, payment procedures, and other related matters.

Delegated Authority. Ex-Im Bank's Delegated Authority program was created to accelerate the process of obtaining a working capital guarantee. An applicant can initiate the application by approaching commercial lenders who are extended this privilege directly rather than meeting with Ex-Im Bank staff. There are four levels of delegated authority lenders, each with specific loan limits per exporter. The lowest lender level is limited to making loans of $2 million per exporter, whereas the highest lender level is able to make loans of up to $10 million per exporter and an aggregate of $150 million. This permits the lenders to commit Ex-Im Bank to a loan with minimal documentation and provides for a reduction in guarantee fees.

Priority Lender Program. Under the Priority Lender Program, a qualified bank is assured faster turnaround for loans of up to $5 million. Qualification for this status includes attendance at Ex-Im Bank seminars, completion of at least two working capital loans, and submission of an annual report. Under this program, Ex-Im Bank guarantees its priority lenders that it will make a decision on a pending loan within 10 business days for standard transactions.

Insurance Programs

Ex-Im Bank offers short-term insurance to cover the preshipment construction period on export transactions. The preshipment period is normally limited to 180 days, but it can be extended depending on certain factors. This type of insurance covers the exporter against the possibility of a buyer declaring bankruptcy and against political risks, such as a foreign government canceling the buyer's import license.

Postshipment Programs

Ex-Im Bank offers numerous programs to support the export of goods and services from the United States. Most of these programs are offered to companies that need short-term (up to one year) support to finance a buyer. There are also medium-term and long-term programs. The major programs in each of these sectors are outlined in the following sections.

Short-Term Credit Insurance

Ex-Im Bank's credit insurance policies provide protection against both the political and commercial risks of a foreign buyer's defaulting on a credit obligation. Policies are available for single or repetitive export sales to individual or multiple buyers. They generally cover from 90 percent to 100 percent of the principal for specified political risks and 90 percent to 98 percent for commercial risks as well as a specified amount of interest.

Short-term policies are used to support the sale of consumer goods, raw materials, and spare parts on terms of up to 180 days and bulk agricultural commodities, consumer durables, and capital goods on terms of up to 360 days. Under medium-term policies, capital goods may be insured for up to seven years, depending upon the contract value. Exporters may obtain receivables financing more easily, because the proceeds of the policy are assignable to banks. Short-term insurance, though, requires that the products be at least 50 percent U.S. origin.

Small Business Policy

The small business policy covers the repayment risks on short-term export sales by U.S. companies that have had a relatively small volume of exports (less than $5 million in credit sales on average over the prior two years). The policy insures 100 percent of specified political risks and 95 percent of all other risks that may lead to default by the buyer, subject to policy conditions. Postmaturity interest, if any, is covered at a rate up to prime minus 0.5 percent. Exporters must agree to include in the policy all their eligible sales. This policy insures short-term credit sales of goods and services. Exporters can assign the policy to a financial institution as collateral for obtaining financing. Another benefit of this policy is that there is no first loss deductible. Premium rates are determined by a schedule. For example, open account sales to a private sector buyer on terms up to 60 days cost 0.65% of the credit invoice, or $65 for every $10,000.

Short-Term Single-Buyer Policy

This policy is custom written for a specified sales contract. Because the policy is structured for single-sale transactions, the standard policy period during which shipments can be made is three months. Ex-Im Bank can issue a policy for up to 12 months to accommodate multiple shipments under a sales contract. Under the policy, there is no requirement to insure a spread of business, thus allowing exporters to insure transactions with or without linking them to bank financing. Coverage applies to credit sales to a foreign buyer, export letters of credit opened by a foreign buyer, or export letters of credit opened by a foreign issuing bank for goods produced in and shipped from the United States during the policy period. Cover is provided for credit terms up to 180 days. On a case-by-case basis, agricultural commodities, capital equipment, and quasi-capital equipment may be insured on terms up to 360 days. Percentages of cover are equalized for commercial and political risks: for sovereign obligors, 100 percent; private-sector and other nonsovereign obligors, 90 percent; LC transactions, 95 percent; bulk agricultural transactions, 98 percent. Premium rates reflect the type of buyer, the credit terms, and the buyer's country. Premium is payable on a monthly basis in arrears, and is based on actual shipments made on credit terms.

Short-Term Multibuyer Policy
Similar to the small business policy described above, this policy is generally written to cover shipments during a one-year period and insures a reasonable spread of an exporter's eligible overseas sales. It provides coverage at lower premiums, helps the exporter to make quicker credit decisions (providing faster service to international buyers), and reduces paperwork. The exporter can obtain financing and can offer competitive credit terms to attract and retain buyers around the globe, even in higher-risk markets. This policy insures short-term sales with repayment terms generally up to 180 days. The policy carries an annual aggregate (cumulative) deductible, and coverage is for 95% of a loss after the deductible is exhausted. For short-term transactions, this coverage applies to the gross invoice amount and, in many cases, to interest at specified rates. Premium is payable monthly in arrears, and is based on an exporter's specific country and credit term mix.

Small Business Environmental Policy
This policy covers the export of products and services designed to control pollution or protect against toxic substances. It carries the same commercial and political risk coverage as the small business policy. There is no minimum annual sales volume to qualify or retain the policy, plus there is no first loss deductible. The maximum term is 180 days, and the policy can be assigned to a financial institution.

Medium-Term Programs
Manufacturers or exporters of capital equipment may find it desirable, or even necessary, to offer extended terms to buyers of capital equipment. Most exporters are not interested in carrying a receivable on their books for several years. Even those that are willing to carry such an asset are rarely willing to do so without some degree of protection. Many exporters have found that they can increase sales by offering extended financing to their buyers. Overseas buyers are often eager to avail themselves of what are

frequently much lower interest rates than they would otherwise be subject to in their own country. The two main sources of medium-term financing are the guarantee and insurance programs offered by ECA and others in the forfait market. Both types of financing are off-balance sheet to the exporter (nonrecourse).

Generally, "medium term" refers to transactions with a maximum maturity of five years. Ex-Im Bank's medium-term programs run from one to seven years. Ex-Im Bank has a number of programs available. Unlike the short-term programs, all of these programs require the buyer to make a 15 percent down payment on the transaction amount. The remaining 85 percent are covered by Ex-Im Bank, depending on the amount of foreign content. If there is no more than 15 percent of foreign content, then Ex-Im Bank covers the entire amount. When foreign content exceeds 15 percent, then Ex-Im Bank can cover only the U.S. content. The maximum foreign content allowed in medium-term transactions is 50 percent. The programs that are of most interest to U.S. exporters are the single-buyer program (insurance), the financial guarantee facility, and direct loans. They are explained in the following sections.

On all medium-term and long-term transactions, repayment of principal and interest is scheduled in semiannual installments, normally beginning six months from the date of product delivery or project completion. Repayment terms usually range between 2 and 10 years, based on the type of product or project and the official Organization for Economic Cooperation and Development's (OECD) country classification.

Repayment terms, customary terms in international trade, generally adhere to the following schedule:

Contract Value	Maximum Repayment Term
Up to $75,000	2 years
$75,000–$149,999	3 years
$150,000–$299,999	4 years
$300,000 or more	5 years (up to 7 years)
Longterm	Over 7 years (not over 12 years)

Ex-Im Bank's guarantee is available for fixed or floating interest rate loans, typically based on the LIBOR. Interest rates for direct loans are based on the lowest rates permitted under the OECD guidelines. Under most circumstances, this rate is the commercial interest reference rate (CIRR), which changes monthly and varies according to the repayment term of the loan as follows:

Repayment Period	Ex-Im Bank's Lending Rate (CIRR)
Up to 5 years	3-year Treasury rate + 1%
5–8.5 years	5-year Treasury rate + 1%
Over 8.5 years	7-year Treasury rate + 1%

Ex-Im Bank charges an up-front exposure fee to the exporter that is assessed on each disbursement of a loan made or guaranteed. Exposure fees vary according to the repayment term of the loan, the classification of the borrower or guarantor (that is government, local bank, or private buyer), and the borrower's country. The exposure fee can be financed in the export loan and thereby passed on to the buyer. An annual commitment fee of 0.5 percent is charged to the borrower on the undisbursed balance of each direct loan. Ex-Im Bank charges the lender a fee of 0.125 percent for the undisbursed amount of each guaranteed loan.

Because Ex-Im Bank must always determine reasonable assurance of repayment when extending credit, it often requires a government, local bank, or foreign branch of a large commercial bank to issue a guarantee. A central bank, finance ministry, or government development bank will provide sovereign guarantees for government buyers. If ample high-quality information can be obtained on a foreign enterprise, Ex-Im Bank will entertain a credit application without outside guarantees.

Medium-Term, Single-Buyer Insurance

This Ex-Im Bank policy is issued in connection with the export of capital equipment. Once the down payment has been deducted, this policy covers 100 percent of the political and commercial risks of default. Unlike short-term insurance, there is no first loss deductible, and the proceeds are assignable to financial institutions. The premium amount is determined by risk.

Repayment Terms.   The financed portion may be in equal installments, payable monthly, quarterly, or semiannually, depending on the total transaction value (see repayment table on previous page). The insurance premium may be included in the financed amount.

How to Apply

  I. Exporter Information
     1. Completed application for approval as a medium-term exporter
     2. Financial statements of exporter for the most recent fiscal year

II. Buyer Information
   1. A credit report from a credit-reporting agency not more than 12 months old
   2. Commercial bank references dated not more than six months from the application
   3. Three years of financial statements plus an interim statement if the fiscal statement is more than nine months old
   4. Two written supplier references

Medium-Term, Financial Guarantee Facility

This program is also designed to help finance the export of capital goods. The main differences between medium-term insurance and a guarantee are listed in Table 3. The same limits of coverage apply as in the single-buyer insurance program. Repayment terms are the same as well, except some transactions may be financed up to seven years. Rather than a premium cost covering the risk, an exposure fee is assessed in the guarantee facility. This fee is determined by risk. Guarantees are generally 0.10 percent to 0.50 percent more expensive than equivalent insurance policies. Content coverage is the same as for insurance. Applying for this type of coverage is more complex than it is with insurance. The various alternatives are explained in the following sections.

How to Apply

There are three ways to apply for Ex-Im Bank guarantees. The simplest and quickest approach is through the Letter of Interest (L/I), followed by the Preliminary Commitment (P/C) and the Final Commitment (A/P).

I. Letter of Interest (L/I)
   This is an application that allows an exporter to obtain an indication from Ex-Im Bank of its willingness to consider financing a given export transaction.
   Issuance of an L/I does not obligate Ex-Im Bank to issue either a P/C or A/P. The benefits of an L/I are:
   1. Useful when bidding or negotiating a contract
   2. Provides an indication of the general eligibility of the buyer and/or the goods or services to be exported
   3. Provides the exporter with advice on the exposure fee (risk-fee), repayment terms, and other program guidelines.
   4. A nonrefundable application fee of $100 to be submitted with the application

II. Preliminary Commitment (P/C)

This application to Ex-Im Bank requests that full details and requirements be provided to the exporter or the borrower for a final commitment to be issued. This step may be bypassed after an L/I has been issued, if the applicant wants to proceed directly for a final commitment (A/P). When Ex-Im Bank issues a P/C, it is always subject to the award of an export contract. There is a $100 application fee unless an L/I application fee has already been paid. In addition to the application fee, there is a processing fee of .10 percent of 1 percent, up to a maximum of $25,000. This fee is rebated only if a final commitment (A/P) is issued. For this reason, an applicant would need to feel very certain that an A/P would be approved. The information requirements for a P/C include full details on:

1. Applicant/Exporter
2. Manufacturer/Producer
3. Purchaser/Borrower/Guarantor
4. Financial statements on borrower and guarantor
5. Related parties
6. Project, products, or services being exported
7. Contract price and repayment terms
8. Competitive information, including company name and country
9. Other supporting information such as invitation to bid and copy of competitor's offer

III. Final Commitment (A/P)

This is an authorization of financing by Ex-Im Bank. An exporter may apply for an A/P only after an export contract has been awarded. Ex-Im Bank will perform a comprehensive evaluation of the transaction and any related issues. There is a $100 application fee if not previously paid for an L/I or P/C. In addition, there is a commitment fee of .125 of 1 percent payable on the undisbursed balance of a guaranteed loan, plus an up-front exposure fee based on repayment terms, type of buyer, and country risk rating. The exposure fee is paid on each disbursement and may be financed. Ex-Im Bank's guarantee is unconditional and transferable. Similar to insurance, a minimum 15 percent down payment is required and U.S. content rules apply. The following detailed information on the transaction is required:

1. Applicant/Buyer
2. Manufacturer/Producer

3. Purchaser/Borrower/Guarantor
4. Financial statements on borrower and guarantor
5. Related parties
6. Project, products, or services being exported
7. Contract price and repayment terms
8. Competitive information, including company name and country
9. Copy of export contract

Long-Term Programs

Transactions requiring more than seven-year financing are considered long-term. In this area, Ex-Im Bank offers guarantees and project-finance programs. The guarantee programs employ the same criteria as for medium-term transactions. To be financed, the minimum transaction amount is $10 million and must be approved by Ex-Im Bank's board of directors.

Tied-Aid Programs

Tied-Aid Capital Projects Fund.   The Ex-Im Bank Tied-Aid Capital Projects Fund counters a foreign-aid donor's use of trade-distorting tied-aid credits. This fund may be used on a case-by-case basis and will be applied only when U.S. exports are directly threatened by foreign tied-aid.

There are additional considerations that may increase the likelihood of tied-aid support. For example, small business exporters receive a high priority. Another factor would be the potential for generating future sales, where the use of tied-aid could "lock-in" a long-term supply relationship. Ex-Im Bank will support sales that combine substantial follow-on market penetration with strong international competitive advantages. To qualify, applicants should have a planning horizon extending beyond the current sale, expect substantial follow-on market penetration, and be willing to engage in energetic price competition against foreign exporters.

Ex-Im Bank has a mandate to meet unfair foreign government financing subsidies. Because many governments subsidize their industries as a matter of policy, low-cost loans or grants are common in the international arena, particularly on larger projects. Ex-Im Bank programs are subject to OECD guidelines for government-supported export financing (see schedules in previous section). Ex-Im Bank is bound by OECD framework agreements; however, it will still attempt to meet foreign competition by offering more attractive terms than would normally be available. Part of the financing offer may be in the form of a grant.

Ex-Im Bank is committed to upholding OECD rules on trade-related aid and supporting the reduction of trade-distorting tied aid. Ex-Im Bank's tied-aid credit is structured as low-rate loans for 100 percent of the export value with a total term of 25 years. The exact interest rate will depend on the concessionality (as defined by the OECD) of the foreign tied-aid credit encountered. The fees are strictly risk-based. Ex-Im Bank's fees reflect pertinent sovereign risks, the financing of 100 percent of export value, and the 25-year term exposure to risk.

Information Requirements

The information requirements for structured trade transactions are more rigorous than for short-term transactions. The reason should be obvious—it is more difficult to determine the likelihood of payment when the repayment terms are extended beyond a short period of time. The documentation requirements are also more extensive than for short-term transactions. In structured trade, both the exporter and the importer are examined. Because this is nonrecourse financing to the seller, any financial institution will want to know the financial capacity and performance history of the seller.

Documentation

As stated earlier, there are numerous documentation requirements, which provide the due diligence and background information to analyze the risks of a transaction. The normal requirements include, but are not limited to, the following:

1. Exporter and importer financial statements
2. Background and history of the exporter and importer
3. Credit reports on the importer
4. Trade references on the importer
5. Copies of purchase orders or contracts
6. Satisfactory guarantor

Financial Analysis

As emphasized in basic and intermediate courses, a rigorous analysis of the importer's financial condition is a requirement for structured trade transactions. In some cases, buyers are approved for direct financing, but often transactions require the intervention of a guarantor. Guarantees are used when it is felt that the risk of repayment directly from the buyer is too great to take. Whether a transaction is completed often depends on whether the buyer can get a guarantee. Before applying for a final commitment under an Ex-Im Bank medium-term transaction, it is critical to determine beforehand that the buyer can get a guarantee, if needed. Otherwise, the exporter will incur a substantial cost for processing the request and it will not be reimbursed if the application is not approved.

Pricing Parameters/Constraints

There is a saying that goes, "Charge what the market will bear." This may be true, but in a global market, the participants need to be cognizant of market conditions, the competition, and pricing constraints. To be competitive in the global market, companies need to know what their competitors are doing and what sources of financing are available. Within these guidelines, every transaction is different and may require different pricing parameters. Lenders vary in their approach to pricing export transactions, but there are standards that everyone should understand. Most lenders, and certainly ECAs, look at country risk first and then at the buyer to determine the appropriate pricing parameters. Some of the key factors in determining price are country rating, buyer rating, ownership, length of the transaction (tenor), and the product being financed.

Country Rating

Most banks and ECAs rate countries on a scale of 1 to 10. The best countries have a "1" rating. Generally, countries rated from 1 to 5 are acceptable credit risks and get the best pricing. Countries rated below 5 carry a higher risk weighting, which increases financing costs. Any country with a 7 rating or higher may find it difficult to arrange financing at any price. It is very possible that a sound company in a difficult country may not be able to attract financing. Thus, a country's risk rating can be advantageous for economic growth or a real deterrent. Factors affecting a country's rating can be related to political, economic, social, religious, and judicial conditions. Depending on the status of a transaction, a negative change in a country's condition can change the pricing or even the viability of the transaction. Therefore, it is very important for exporters, lenders, and ECAs always to monitor country conditions when considering a transaction.

Buyer Rating

Just like with countries, buyers are also rated. The ratings are usually the same, 1–10, with "1" being the best. If a buyer has a strong rating (1–4), there is normally less need to consider a guarantor. Guarantees are usually required when the buyer's risk rating is 5 or higher. Every lender calculates the "risk of repayment." Unfortunately, it is generally true that the higher the rating, the risk of repayment is also greater. Buyers are normally rated based on a combination of factors, including a review of financial statements, credit reports, bank references, trade references, company history, and the deal structure.

Ownership

This is a key factor in determining risk and pricing parameters. There are five key levels of ownership that are reviewed: Is the company privately owned, publicly traded, a sovereign governmental agency, a nonsovereign governmental agency, or a private financial institution? The ECAs like Ex-Im Bank have developed a rating matrix based upon the type of borrower/guarantor. The best ratings go to sovereign government agencies and then to banks.

Tenor

The length of a transaction also has a lot to do with the cost of the financing. Generally, short-term transactions are much less expensive than medium- to long-term deals. The main reason for this differentiation is that it is more difficult to assess the likelihood of repayment on a medium-term transaction compared with a short-term one. Most export financing is of the short-term nature (one year).

Product Classification / Service

Depending on the standard industrial classification (SIC) of the product being shipped or the service being provided, a product may be limited in the length of the financing. Generally, manufactured product and services are only financed on a short-term basis. Capital equipment can be financed for periods greater than one year, depending on the dollar value of the shipment.

Taking all of these factors into account, a lender or export credit agency will calculate an appropriate risk-weighted price. This price must be acceptable to the buyer who will ultimately be paying for the financing. Many transactions are never concluded because of price constraints that the buyer is unwilling to pay. To be successful in this business, exporters should find out early in the process what the anticipated documentation and pricing structures will be and discuss them with the buyer.

Cost of Capital and Capital Structure

Sometimes both exporters and importers are not aware of how pricing formulas can impact their cost of capital. In some cases, a company's capital structure may be a detriment to getting a good financing rate or documentation structure. If a borrower is poorly capitalized, this might require a guarantee, which could increase the costs to an unacceptable level. Likewise, if a company uses cash-basis accounting procedures, it is unlikely to receive the most attractive financing structure, because lenders cannot base their risk of repayment on only the financial statements of the company. Guarantees of the principal shareholders will generally be required, as well. As a result, this might make the financing unattractive to the company.

Competitive Issues

There are a number of competitive issues that need to be mentioned in export finance transactions. Any one or all of them may have an impact on successful completion of a transaction.

Shipping Terms

When quoting a price for products or services, a company must understand how to quote a price properly using International Commercial Terms (INCOTERMS 2000). If it is a bid situation, everyone should be submitting a quotation based on the same terms.

Method of Shipment and Ship Lines

How product is shipped has a real impact on cost and price. In addition, most ECAs restrict shipment to certain carriers. Depending on logistical considerations, this could negatively impact a company's competitive position.

Unfair Market Practices

Some companies and countries may try unfair financing proposals. Exporters should always be aware of this. These practices can be offset by "tied-aid" support from a local ECA. Under most ECAs and under U.S. laws, it is illegal to pay bribes or knowingly be involved in such actions.

Tenors

In a competitive environment, an exporter can always try to be creative. One way to be creative is to offer different financing options to a buyer based on repayment terms. If the buyer is looking for two-year financing, but an exporter is able to offer three-year terms at the same rate, then the buyer may find the second option more appealing.

Application and Approval Procedures

There are specific application and approval procedures for each Ex-Im Bank program. Generally, a one- to four-page application form needs to be completed by the exporter. Depending on whether approval is being sought for short- or medium-term transactions, the approval requirements vary. Listed below are the general approval requirements for both short- and medium-term insurance transactions.

Short-Term Credit Standards[11]

Exporter Credit Standards
1. Favorable credit report dated within six months of the application
2. Dun & Bradstreet Paydex greater than or equal to 50
3. For supplier credits, basic financial information that provides reasonable assurance that the proposed transaction is not disproportionate in scope and scale relative to the exporter's financial wherewithal and nature of its business operations
4. For qualified small business exporters requesting the Enhanced Assignment of Policy Proceeds, the standards listed in Table E of the policy

Importer Credit Standards
1. Domicile acceptable according to Ex-Im Bank's Country Limitation Schedule
2. Not suspended or barred from doing business with the U.S. government
3. No unresolved payment issues on debts, guarantees, or insurance with the Ex-Im Bank

Medium-Term Credit Standards[12]

Nonfinancial Institutions Without Market Indications
1. Domicile acceptable according to Country Limitation Schedule
2. Not suspended or barred from doing business with the U.S. government
3. No unresolved payment issues on debts, guarantees, or insurance with the Ex-Im Bank
4. In the same general line of business at least three years
5. Credit report and creditor bank reference contains no material adverse information
6. Audited or unaudited statements adequately disclose financial condition and were prepared according to accounting principles

---

[11] The information on short-term credit standards is extracted from the United States Export-Import Bank's website at www.exim.gov. The information is available in document number EIB99-09 (10/99).

[12] The information on medium-term credit standards is extracted from the United States Export-Import Bank's website at www.exim.gov. The information is available in document number EBD-M-39 (11/99).

that afford a reasonable basis for reliance on the information provided
   - Auditor's opinion is either (a) unqualified or (b) qualified with respect to amounts and circumstances not considered material to creditworthiness
7. Performance criteria are met, which include the following:
   - Positive operating profit and net income in each of last two fiscal years
   - Positive cash from operations in last fiscal year
   - EBITDA/debt service (including Ex-Im Bank debt if more than 25 percent of total debt) is at least 1.5 for last fiscal year
   - Total liabilities (excluding Ex-Im Bank debt) do not exceed 1.75 times tangible net worth at end of last fiscal year
   - Ex-Im Bank exposure does not exceed 40 percent of tangible net worth at end of last fiscal year
   - Interim statements disclose no material adverse change in financial condition

Financial Institutions Without Market Indications
1. Domicile acceptable according to Country Limitation Schedule
2. Not suspended or barred from doing business with U.S. government
3. No unresolved payment issues on debts to or guaranteed or insured by Ex-Im Bank
4. In the same general line of business at least three years
5. Creditor bank reference contains no material adverse information
6. Audited statements adequately disclose financial condition and were prepared according to accounting principles that afford a reasonable basis for reliance on the information provided
   - Auditor's opinion is either (a) unqualified or (b) qualified with respect to amounts and circumstances not considered material to creditworthiness
7. Performance criteria, which include the following, are met:
   - Net income in last fiscal year is at least one percent of average of total assets at end of last fiscal years
   - Liquid assets are at least 10 percent of total assets at end of last fiscal year
   - Loan loss reserves are at least 80 percent of nonperforming loans at end of last fiscal year
   - Borrowed funds are less than 100 percent of net loans at end of last fiscal year

8. Shareholders' equity is at least five percent of total assets at end of last fiscal year
9. Ex-Im Bank exposure does not exceed 40 percent of shareholders' equity at the end of the last fiscal year
10. Interim statements disclose no material adverse change in financial condition

Corporate and Financial Institution Guarantees
1. If primary source of repayment is a start-up company, a guarantor that meets applicable standards is required.
2. If the ability to service debt is materially dependent on cash flow from a major expansion or a new line of business, a guarantor that meets applicable standards is required.
3. If more than 25 percent of sales in the last fiscal year were to a related or commonly owned company, a guarantee of the related or commonly owned company is required.
4. If more than 25 percent of purchases of primary source of repayment in last fiscal year were from a related or commonly owned company, a guarantee of the related or commonly owned company is required.

Personal Guarantees
1. For financial institutions, personal guarantees are not required.
2. For nonfinancial institutions with sales revenue of at least $50 million in last fiscal year, personal guarantees are not required.
3. For nonfinancial institutions with sales revenue of less than $50 million in last fiscal year, personal guarantees are required of individuals with ownership interest exceeding 50 percent.

Security Interests and Covenants
1. Guarantees are not required with the exception of transactions involving the export of aircraft.
2. Standard special conditions are required for aircraft transactions.

Credit Availability and Capacity Issues

The availability of credit and capacity are two different but interrelated issues. It makes sense to discuss capacity before availability. Capacity will be defined as the desired level of credit commitment a financial institution or ECA has in a specific country. This will also be described as the "aggregate credit limit" or "country limit." It is within this country limit that a financial institution or ECA determines separate credit limits for individual banks, government entities, or direct borrowers. Thus, credit availability is defined as the amount of the aggregate credit limit available at any time for a potential borrower.

Capacity

It is crucial for exporters to monitor capacity in a country. If the buyer's country is an active user of credit, an ECA may run out of country limit. When this occurs, transactions are paused until capacity becomes available. Capacity can be curtailed for negative reasons as well. A country may incur economic difficulty or another condition that creates an atmosphere of instability. An ECA may temporarily close capacity on the basis of these and other factors. In addition, commercial banks monitor country conditions and often follow the lead taken by ECAs in opening or closing capacity. This can have a positive or negative impact on credit markets.

Credit Availability

Within the overall country limit established by an ECA like Ex-Im Bank, separate limits will be approved for specific institutions. These individual limits or the aggregate limit can, at times, be used actively. It is important to monitor both limits, because they need to be available in order for a financial transaction to be approved. If a medium-term transaction is being contemplated with a specific institution, but there is no availability under its credit line, then an alternative borrower/guarantor may need to be used. This could significantly alter the transaction structure and pricing. At times, the credit limit of the borrowing entity is open, but the country limit is fully used. This means that the transaction will not be completed until country limit is made available.

Portfolio Management and Asset Allocation

As in any business, ECAs and financial institutions balance their appetite for risk based upon industry characteristics and portfolio concentration. Most financial institutions focus on specific industries. Within those industries, they try to spread and diversify risks among numerous transactions and various companies.

Portfolio Management

Export credit agencies and banks determine the type of transactions that "make sense" and that have a "reasonable risk of repayment." Within these parameters, decisions are made to handle short- or medium-term transactions or a combination of the two. Once the portfolio sectors are identified, then the ECA or bank sets limits for each type of transaction. These limits are used to manage the portfolio.

Asset Allocation

In building a portfolio of transactions, it is important to determine which transactions are going to get priority. This is the process of asset allocation. Among commercial banks, one important criterion used to allocate assets is whether the exporter is a client of the bank. Many banks, regardless of how the transaction may be priced, will not take medium-term export risk for nonclients. Banks are also reluctant to work in certain industries. These factors are important to know before approaching a bank for financial support. By contrast, ECAs are normally involved in helping all sectors accomplish their export goals. In this regard, they are considered the "lenders of last resort." Thus, in many cases, Ex-Im Bank will require exporters to provide proof that a bank has turned them down before it will support a transaction.

Overseas Private Investment Corporation

The Overseas Private Investment Corporation (OPIC) is an important resource for exporters involved in third-world countries, especially if some form of temporary investment is needed in the export or project. Established as a development agency of the U.S. government in 1971, OPIC's activities include insurance, loans, loan guarantees, a variety of investor services, and a special program to protect contractors and exporters. Investment insurance is OPIC's largest program and covers risks such as currency inconvertibility, expropriation, and political violence. The coverage can include loss of income as well as tangible property loss and frequently involves project financing as well as cross-border leasing. Whereas most OPIC activities relate to medium- or long-term activities, the Contractor and Exporter Insurance program is specialized to help these parties in the case of wrongful government actions, such as disputes pertaining to the underlying contract and payments for same, wrongful calling of standby letters of credit for performance or bid bonds, or loss of assets due to inconvertibility, confiscation, or political violence. In all of these areas, OPIC's coverage is for 90 percent of the loss.

The Overseas Private Investment Corporation's second major activity is providing medium- to long-term funding for new ventures or the expansion or modernization of existing, successful ventures involving at least 25 percent equity or management participation by U.S. businesses. Rather than relying on foreign government guaranties, OPIC's limited recourse financing looks for repayment from revenues generated by the project. This allows OPIC to finance projects in countries where conventional financial institutions often are reluctant or unable to lend on such a basis. Thus, OPIC does not provide concessional financing, because it is oriented to the private sector and to projects that amortize themselves on an economic basis, however creative.

The Overseas Private Investment Corporation serves small- and medium-sized companies through its Small and Medium Enterprise (SME) Department, which houses the Small Business Center (SBC). Also, OPIC has a Structured Finance Department to meet the requirements of its largest customers. Eligibility for a particular program is based on a series of defined criteria, which are listed in the following table:[13]

Eligibility Criteria for OPIC Programs

	Small Business Center	Small and Medium Enterprise	Structured Finance
If the sponsor is a corporation:	U.S. corporation with *less than* *$35 million* in revenues	U.S. corporation with *less than* *$250 million* in revenues	U.S. corporation with *greater than* *$250 million* in revenues
If the sponsor is an individual or investment entity:	Individuals or investment entities with *less than $27 million* in equity	Individuals or investment entities with *less than $67 million* in equity	Individuals or investment entities with *greater than $67 million* in equity
Is the project in the oil and gas Industry?	No	No	Yes
Does the project have serious environmental implications?	No	Yes	Yes

[13] "OPIC Lending Programs". Overseas Private Investment Corporation. May 2005. Accessed from http://www.opic.gov/Finance in July 2005.

Small and Medium Enterprise Department

The SME and the SBC were established specifically to address the needs of small and medium-sized American companies in order to ease their entry into new markets. Recognizing the financing needs facing many small businesses, the Center is committed to considering all applications within a 60-day period.

In certain cases, clients may choose between the SME and SBE programs. Features distinguishing the two programs are as follows:[14]

Comparison of OPIC SBC and SME Programs

	SBC Program	SME Program
OPIC Spread (on top of OPIC Cost of Funds)	6%–7%	2%–5%
Commitment Fees	NA	0.5%–1%
Facility Fees	1%–2%	1%–3%
Maintenance Fees	$5,000–$10,000 per annum	$10,000–$20,000 per annum
Time from completed application to Legal Documentation Closing	60 days	90–180 days
Collateral and Security	Guaranty of Sponsor Pledge of Shares Reserve Accounts Some assets in the U.S.	Guaranty of Sponsor Pledge of Shares Reserve Accounts Lien on Project Assets

Small Business Center

The SBC finance program loan amounts for overseas investments range from $100,000 to $10 million with terms from 3 to 15 years. Interest rates are capped at seven percent above the Direct Loan Discount Rate, which is set by the U.S. Treasury. In addition, there may be a one-time facility fee of up to two percent and an annual maintenance fee not to exceed one percent of the outstanding balance of the loan. Although the eligible U.S. small business must own at least 25 percent of the overseas project, OPIC may be able to finance up to 65 percent of the total project costs.[15] The following

---

[14] "Comparison of SBC and SME Programs". Overseas Private Investment Corporation. June 2004. Accessed from http://www.opic.gov/finance/compareSBCSME.htm in July 2005.

[15] "OPIC Supports U.S. Small Business". Overseas Private Investment Corporation. May 2005. Accessed from http://www.opic.gov/smallbiz/sb_center.htm in July 2005.

vignette highlights the processes undergone by Prefabricados y Modulares de Monterrey (PyMM), a manufacturer of prefabricated affordable and quality housing that sought SBC financing from OPIC.

Prefabricados y Modulares de Monterrey and OPIC

Located in Monterey, Mexico, and as a wholly-owned subsidiary of Modular Prefab USA, PyMM was founded in May 2000 to serve the low-income housing needs of the state of Nuevo Leon. With over 90 years of combined experience in the construction industry in the United States, PyMM management appeared to be a perfect fit for the Mexican market, which was experiencing a rapidly growing economy and population but severe shortage of affordable and safe housing. In the state of Tamaulipas alone, the housing need exceeded 90,000 units.

The PyMM management had a clear plan to meet the needs of the underserved low-income housing market, but to meet the need sufficiently, the expansion of facilities was necessary. Prefabricados y Modulares de Monterrey's current plant was capable of producing about five houses per day. The acquisition of additional equipment, however, could increase the current production to eight houses per day. A follow-up expansion could increase production capacity even further, to 12 houses per day. Clearly, the company's expansion strategy required capital expenditure investments and additional working capital. Although PyMM had been operating successfully in Mexico for over five years, it simply did not have the resources to pursue the expansion alone.

With financial advice from Interlink Capital Strategies (www.i-caps.com), however, PyMM was able to submit a 10-year, $10 million long-term debt financing application to OPIC. The application included a financing form, business plan, financial statements of the sponsor and project, description of ownership structure, financial projections of future operations, commercial and financial agreements related to the project, sponsor disclosure reports for each entity considered to be a sponsor, and feasibility, marketing, and environmental studies.

The $10 million application was approved for disbursement, and PyMM expects to increase production to 2,000 units per year. Subsequent capital expenditures investments will allow the company to reach its target production of 3,000 units per year within the next two years. By partnering with Infonavit, an existing Mexican real-estate program, PyMM is currently developing several subdivisions simultaneously to better ensure that the demand for affordable housing in Mexico can be met.

Project-Finance Loans

In addition to SBC and SME loans, OPIC also offers project-finance loans, which average about $1 million, and guarantees that can be up to $250 million. The borrower of a project-finance-style loan is typically an overseas entity that is at least 25 percent owned by an OPIC-eligible U.S. business. The term of the loan, depending on the attributes of the project being financed, generally spans between 3 and 15 years. The primary source of repayment for the project-finance-style loan must be the overseas project's own operating cash flow. The collateral, also offered as a secondary source of repayment, could be located in the host country or in the United States. Finally, if the project meets predefined physical, operational, legal, and financial tests, the guaranties may be reduced or eliminated.

SME's Franchise Loans

The Overseas Private Investment Corporation also provides franchise loans to operations that involve at least 25 percent ownership or "significant involvement" by a U.S. business. The criteria defining "significant involvement" by a U.S. business are detailed as follows:

1. The business concepts and systems employed by the franchisee were originally developed by the U.S. small-business franchisor.
2. A long-term franchise agreement is in effect among the U.S. franchisor, the local in-country master franchisor, and the franchisee.
3. Local use of the U.S. franchisor's trademark or brand name is evident.
4. The U.S. franchisor is at risk for payment of franchise fees.

Franchise loans generally range from a three- to eight-year term and fund between $100,000 and $4 million. To meet OPIC's underwriting conditions, franchise transactions must be financially sound, as indicated by an acceptable debt-to-equity ratio, fixed charge ratio, and debt service coverage ratio, among others. Furthermore, personal guaranties from franchisee owners are required for all loans, and start-up franchisees are eligible for financing if cash flow independent of the franchisee operation is used to service the OPIC loan until the franchisee operation is capable of servicing the loan from its own cash flow.

Information required for the application from the U.S. franchisor and the franchisee-borrower is as listed:[16]

Items Required from the U.S. Franchisor
1. Offering circular from U.S. franchisor for most recent two years
2. Financial statements of U. S. franchisor for most recent three years
3. Financial criteria of U.S. franchisor for awarding a franchise
4. Financial criteria of U.S. franchisor for permitting expansion
5. Description of U.S. franchisor's approval process for suppliers of franchisee
6. Description of due diligence undertaken by the U.S franchisor on the franchisee

Materials Required from the Franchisee-Borrower
1. Financial statements of borrower for past three years.
2. Franchise agreement.
3. Territorial development agreement, if applicable.
4. Borrower's business plan.
5. Financial projections (electronic version and printout of the projections).
6. Existing leases of borrower (expansion only); if these leases are not in English, a summary of key terms of existing leases. Key terms include: when the lease expires, the annual rent, how any rent escalation is calculated, name of lessee, and name of lessor.
7. New leases of borrower for the project; if these leases are not in English, a summary of key terms of leases for project (see number 6 for list of key terms).
8. List of borrower's key suppliers and length of time those suppliers have been approved by the U.S. franchisor.

---

[16] "Franchise Loans". Overseas Private Investment Corporation. June 2004. Accessed from http://www.opic.gov/finance/SME/sme_Products/sme_franloan.htm in July 2005.

9. Description of the construction arrangements and how construction risk is allocated.

10. List of the training courses that owner has completed with U.S. franchisor.

11. Copies of permits and licenses that are required for the borrower's operation.

12. Completed OPIC application (cross link to application).

If franchisee is a start-up, the following information must also be provided:

13. Identify source of loan repayment that is independent from the franchise operation.

14. Provide supporting information on the independent source of repayment.

Contact:

Overseas Private Investment Corporation
1100 New York Avenue, NW
Washington DC 20527
E-mail: smallbiz@opic.gov
Local Phone: (202) 336-8700
Fax: (202) 336-8701

CHAPTER 10

PROJECT FINANCE

This financing technique is generally used for large projects. Lenders give as much consideration to the project's current stream of revenue and future profits as they do to present liquid assets of the borrower or other financial institution guarantees. Project financing is especially difficult to arrange and is usually supported by government financing agencies such as the Ex-Im Bank. In addition, U.S. exporters can sometimes obtain financing from another country's ECAs for products or projects that have high-percentage origin content from that country.

Project financing is typically for capital-intensive greenfield projects involving construction, testing, and start-up periods. Furthermore, the repayment of scheduled debt service in any one period is often heavily dependent upon realization of projected cash flows, budget costs, scheduled milestones, and performance criteria in the same period. Other familiar characteristics of project financing include the following:

- Lack full recourse to the sponsor, equity holders, or other third party for the full term of the exposure
- Secured by various combinations of contracts and contract rights, partnership agreements or the like, permits and/or real property, and a pledge of shares
- Involve the long-term production or processing of a commodity product in a facility that is typically very high cost; to achieve adequate equity returns, long-term financing is required

Risks and Mitigants

Although many characteristics of project financing are deal specific, there are some generic ones. A number of general areas of risk include economic viability, loan repayment, construction, regulatory risk, operations and maintenance, and foreign exchange risks. Specific measures that can be taken to mitigate such risks are as follows:

Economic Risk

1. There should be a long-term sales agreement for the project's output that matches the project's cost structure such that the project sufficiently mitigates volume and price risk.

2. The production cost should be competitive with other resources available to the purchaser, including other projects and, if applicable, the purchaser's own production.

3. The revenue source should be "friendly" and have willingly entered into the purchase contract as a result of an arms-length negotiation absent regulatory or other pressure/coercion.

4. The developer/sponsor should have substantial strategic and financial interest in the outcome of the project.

5. The lender must be prepared to accept the credit risk of the power purchaser. Its ability and willingness to meet its contractual obligations should be within the risk-tolerance limits of the lender.

Repayment/Refinancing Risk

One of the most important factors of successful project financing is the quality and certainty of project cash flow. As a rule of thumb, lenders would like to see averages of pro forma debt-service coverage ratios between 1.25 and 1.5. Furthermore, a debt-service reserve fund (DSRF) should be established and contain a cover for at least three months (preferably six months), and principal and interest should be funded initially as part of the last construction draw. In certain circumstances, a letter of credit may also be acceptable in lieu of the DSRF. Other possible requirements to mitigate repayment risks are as follows:

1. A distribution block that provides for the retention of cash flow in the project when the DSCR falls below 1.25

2. Typical sensitivity analysis that includes tests of interest rate change for floating loans, increase of operating and managing fees, devaluation and inflation, price change, volume changes of output and input, decrease of capacity and/or availability, and a break-even case

Construction Risk

Construction risk includes exposure to completion delays, cost overruns, production shortage, and failure to meet efficiency standards, among others. Lenders generally require that this risk be covered by an EPC contract and/or sponsor support. Construction quality can affect the ability of the project to repay its debt. Because construction is arguably the most critical stage of a project's life, it is imperative to focus on means to mitigate its risks.

Some methods follow:

1. The primary construction contract should be of a turnkey nature
   and provide for (a) a guaranteed maximum price, (b) completion by
   a certain date, and (c) performance and delay liquidated damages
   (20 percent to 35 percent total) sufficient to compensate the project
   for performance and schedule shortfalls.
2. The construction contractor should be reputable, experienced,
   and capable of the task as well as have sufficient financial
   resources to meet the construction contract obligation. The contractor
   should provide performance bonds from a high-rated agency.
3. Completion tests in both the construction contract and credit agreement should be adequately designed to ensure operating capability
   consistent with the project's contractual obligations as well as the
   operating assumptions incorporated into the underwriting projections.
4. The construction contract should include warranties, typically lasting
   from one to two years, depending on the technology.
5. Technology should be standard, time-tested, low-risk, have minimal
   experimental features, and meet all environmental standards (noise,
   emissions, etc.) consistent with the plant's permits.
6. The construction schedule and budget should be detailed,
   verifiable, provide for reasonable contingencies for both cost
   overruns and delays, and be generally consistent with good
   engineering practices.
7. The project should have a good relationship with its host
   community.
8. Other mitigants include delay in start-up insurance to cover
   insurable events that cause delays, contingent equity from sponsors
   to cover cost overruns, and contractor completion guarantee.
9. An independent engineer (IE) should sign off on the technical
   feasibility, budget, and schedule of the project prior to construction.
   During the construction period, the IE should monitor the
   construction progress on a monthly basis and sign off on a
   construction progress report prior to each draw.

Operating Risk

Exposure to lower-than-expected operating performance, such as con-
strained availability, operation interruptions, and equipment failures, is often
the greatest barrier to project-finance success. Operating risk will affect the

cash flows available to serve project debt, which must withstand downside scenarios. Specific means to address operating risk are as detailed:

1. The operator should be experienced, reputable, and capable of operating the project.
2. Operation and maintenance (O&M) costs and capital expenditures should be verifiable, reasonably estimated, and sufficiently detailed and conservative.
3. The O&M costs should be largely fixed by long-term contract on terms consistent with the output contract such that the project does not accept significant cost/revenue mismatch.
4. There should be adequate property and casualty and business interruption insurance to cover insurable events.

Regulatory Risk

To mitigate regulatory risks associated with project finance, the following must be kept in mind:

1. All necessary permits and approvals for construction, operation, and enforceability of contracts should have been obtained or be easily obtainable if customarily received at a later date.
2. The long-term sales agreement should not contain a regulatory out clause that allows for reduction in the contract's offtake amount or price before loan payout.
3. Changes in law provisions in the contract may allow the project contractor to pass along to the purchaser increases in costs according to the terms of the sales contract.

Credit Review of Project Participants

In the credit review process, lenders examine project participants' knowledge of project technology and experience, particularly with projects that have been developed and operated successfully. In addition to experience, developers and sponsors should have sufficient financial, managerial, and technical capability to resolve difficulties that are likely to arise in the course of project development. The following list details specific criteria expected from project participants:

Borrower: Able to support the project structure and provide the cash flow necessary for repayment.

Offtaker: Reliable to service its contractual obligations as the ultimate source of project income.

Sponsors: Capable to meet their equity funding obligations and/or contingent obligations. (Lenders typically seek a parent guarantee in support of these obligations or an L/C if the parent is of less-than-acceptable creditworthiness.)

Construction contractor: Able to ensure the timely and on-budget completion of project's construction and reliable operation with parent guarantees, retainage withheld from progress payments, and a liquidity L/C.

Operator: Competent to provide operational efficiency and reliability. (As operators' damages are generally limited to the fees earned in any year, lenders rely on the operators' track record and the incentive structure of the O&M contract to wage operators' competency.)

Other lenders: Able to fund on-time and sufficient amounts to complete construction; need to ensure that other lender "conditions precedent to disbursement" are reviewed and initial risks to nondisbursement at the first and ongoing disbursement dates are sufficiently mitigated.

CHAPTER 11

COUNTERTRADE[17]

Countertrade is its very own world. Although statistics vary wildly as to the percentage of world trade it represents, there is more of it than one would imagine. With roots in the ancient trade concept of bartering, countertrade does not really involve financing, as it is the exchange of one product for another product. In some transactions, a buyer does not have money available to pay for product that it needs. In lieu of making a monetary payment, the buyer will offer the seller another form of payment. This is usually in the form of another product. To complete a sale of this type, the seller must be very knowledgeable about the product it is receiving and must arrange the sale of that product carefully before agreeing to the transaction.

For transactions in the developing world, including parts of Eastern and Central Europe and Latin America, countertrade is a necessary fact of life. As world-debt crises and exchange-rate volatility have made ordinary trade financing very risky, many countries in the developing world cannot obtain the trade credit or financial assistance necessary to afford desired imports. Heavily indebted nations, faced with the possibility of not being able to afford imports, resort to countertrade to maintain product inflow.

Another benefit of countertrade is that it permits the covert reduction of prices and therefore allows firms and governments to circumvent price and exchange controls. Particularly in commodity markets with operative cartel arrangements, such as oil or agriculture, this benefit may be very useful to a producer. For example, by using oil as a countertraded product for industrial equipment, a surreptitious discount (by using a higher price for the acquired products) may expand market share. In a similar fashion, the countertrading of products at higher prices than their economic value has the potential to mask dumping activities.

Countertrade is also often viewed by firms and nations alike as an excellent mechanism to gain entry into new markets. When a producer believes that marketing is not its strong suit, particularly in product areas that face strong international competition, it often sees countertrade as useful. The producer often hopes that the party receiving the goods will serve as a new

[17] Section is adapted from Michael R. Czinkota and Ilkka A. Ronkainen. "Countertrade". *International Marketing, Seventh Edition*. Mason, OH: Thomson, 2004. 500–505.

distributor, opening up new international marketing channels and ultimately expanding the original market. Conversely, markets with high demand and little cash can provide major opportunities for firms if they are willing to accept countertrade. A firm that welcomes countertrade welcomes new buyers and sets itself apart from the competition.

Another advantage of countertrade is that it can provide stability for long-term sales. For example, if a firm is tied to a countertrade agreement, it will need to source the product from a particular supplier, whether or not it wants to do so. This stability is often valued very highly because it eliminates, or at least reduces, vast swings in demand and thus allows for better planning.

In spite of all these apparent benefits of countertrade, there are strong economic arguments against this activity. These arguments are based mainly on efficiency grounds. As economist Paul Samuelson stated, "Instead of there being a double coincidence of wants, there is likely to be a want of coincidence; so that, unless a hungry tailor happens to find an undraped farmer, who has both food and a desire for a pair of pants, neither can make a trade."[18] Instead of trade balances being settled on a multilateral basis, with surpluses from one country being balanced by deficits with another, countertrade requires that accounts must now be settled on a country-by-country or even transaction-by-transaction basis. Trade then results only from the ability of two parties or countries to purchase specified goods from one another rather than from competition. As a result, uncompetitive goods may be marketed. In consequence, the ability of countries and their industries to adjust structurally to more efficient production may be restricted. Countertrade can therefore be seen as eroding the quality and efficiency of production and as lowering world consumption. These economic arguments notwithstanding, however, countries and companies increasingly see countertrade as an alternative that may be flawed but worthwhile to undertake.

Countertrade—Pepsi and Caterpillar

Countertrade, the pivot of Stone Age economics, is more vital in today's business transactions than you may think. It is estimated that 65 percent of Fortune 500 companies—including PepsiCo, Pizza Hut, Casio, General Electric, IBM, 3M, Caterpillar, and

---

[18] Paul Samuelson, *Economics*, 11th ed. (New York: McGraw-Hill, 1980), 260.

Xerox—engage in some form of countertrade. In the U.S. market alone, countertrade is a $16 billion industry and accounts for nearly 33 percent of all trades.[19]

One of the most famous examples of a successful countertrade deal was an arrangement between Pepsi-Cola and the Soviet Union that financed the introduction and expansion of Pepsi into the Soviet Union. In place of hard currency payment for Pepsi, the Soviets granted Pepsi North American 10-year distribution and marketing rights for Stolichnaya Vodka. Pepsi essentially exchanged Pepsi-Cola for vodka, which it imported into the United States. The aggressive marketing for Stolichnaya led to the creation of the premium vodka market.[20]

In another case, Caterpillar Incorporated, a market leader in construction equipment manufacturing, spearheaded a three-legged countertrade transaction to complete a sale in Venezuela. Because the Venezuelan client, an iron ore mining facility, lacked cash and credit reserves to pay for mining equipment, Caterpillar provided the client with the equipment upfront, given that the client would sell the mined iron to one of Caterpillar's European suppliers. The supplier, in turn, paid Caterpillar directly for the iron and refined the iron into steel, the chief material in Caterpillar equipment.[21]

Types of Countertrade

Although no two writers seem to agree on the exact names for the various forms of countertrade, the author of this book believes that five general forms can best describe countertrade in all its varieties. These are (1) barter, (2) compensation, (3) counterpurchase, (4) buyback, and (5) offset. Each of the types of countertrade is detailed in the following paragraphs and their relationship is illustrated by Exhibit 2.

---

[19] Sanjay Moolchandani, "Now, Swap Your Old Mobile For a Music System," *The Economic Times,* 22 July 2005, accessed from http://economictimes.indiatimes.com/articleshow/msid-1179195,curpg-2.cms 18 August 2005.

[20] Dan West, "Countertrade: An Innovative Approach to Marketing," Barter News, 1996, accessed from http://www.barternews.com/approach_marketing.htm 18 August 2005.

[21] Author interview with Wayne Cooper, Treasurer of Global Offset and Countertrade Association, 17 August 2005.

Exhibit 2   Different Forms of Countertrade[22]

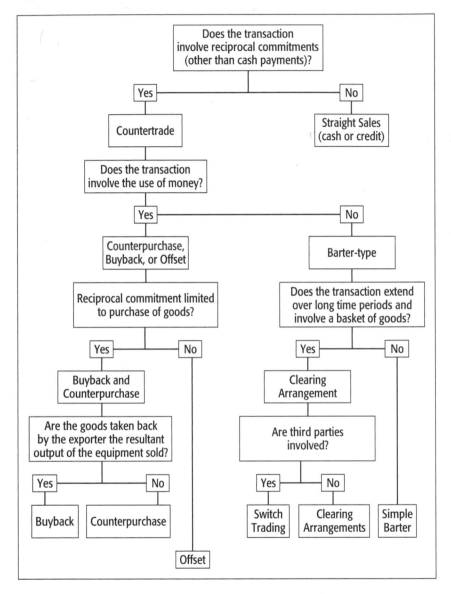

---

[22] Adapted from Jean-Francois Hennart, "Some Empirical Dimensions of Countertrade". *Journal of International Business Studies* 21 (No. 2, 1990): 245.

Barter

Barter, the earliest form of trade, is still in use today, both domestically and internationally. It is characterized by a direct exchange of goods of equal value. Historically, countertrade was conducted mainly in the form of barter, which is a direct exchange of goods of approximately equal value, with no money involved. These transactions were the very essence of business at times when no money existed or was available. Over time, money emerged to unlink transactions from individual parties and permit greater flexibility in trading activities.

Repeatedly, however, we can see returns to the barter system as a result of economic circumstances. For example, because of tight financial constraints during its initial years of operation after 1789, Georgetown University charged its students part of the tuition in foodstuffs and required students to participate in the construction of university buildings. Another example of modern-day bartering was during periods of high inflation in Europe in the 1920s, when goods such as bread, meat, and gold were seen as much more useful and secure than paper money, which decreased in real value every hour.

Compensation

Compensation is a modernized version of countertrade in which both of the products exchanged are valued in specified currencies and invoiced in those currencies. Thus, the transaction may be of unequal value for each side, and payment may be partly in product and partly in currency. Even though the transactions need not take place simultaneously, they are all covered by a single contract, which enjoys a factor of simplicity for smaller businesses but which can also make the deal a bit unwieldy.

Counterpurchase

Counterpurchase, also known as parallel barter, accounts for the largest dollar volume of countertrade today, but it is better designed for medium-to-large corporations or established countertrade firms than it is for smaller businesses. Two contracts are signed and delivery, invoicing, and payment are carried out independently for each transaction. The arrangements sometimes cover periods of as much as five years. Frequently, the exchange is not of precisely equal value; therefore, some amount of cash will be involved.

Buyback

Buyback is similar to counterpurchase and best describes many turnkey projects, although it is not necessarily limited to large projects. One party agrees to supply technology or equipment that enables the other party to produce goods with which the price of the supplied products or technology is repaid. An important consideration in such arrangements is the quality of the product the turnkey project's plant will produce. It is important that the contractor-builder retains some control over supervision of the plant or equipment operations and over employee training to ensure the quality of the product it will later be obliged to sell. One example of such a buyback arrangement is an agreement entered into by Levi Strauss and Hungary. The company transferred the know-how and the Levi's trademark to Hungary. A Hungarian firm began producing Levi's products. Some of the output is sold domestically, and the rest is marketed in Western Europe by Levi Strauss, in compensation for the know-how.

Offset

Another key form of barter arrangement is called offset. This is the industrial compensation mandated by governments when purchasing defense-related goods and services in order to offset the effect of this purchase on the balance of payments. Offsets can include coproduction, licenses production, subcontractor production, technology transfer, or overseas investment. Typically, to secure the sale of military equipment, the selling companies have to offset the cost of the arms through investment in nonrelated industries. The offsets frequently reach or exceed the price of the defense equipment, to the delight of the buyer, but often to the chagrin of the home country government of the selling firms. For example, U.S. weapons exporters alone are estimated to complete about $1 billion to $3 billion annually in defense offset transactions, which, according to some estimates, may strengthen foreign competitors and adversely affect employment.

Preparing for Countertrade

Early on in the countertrade process, a firm needs to decide whether it wishes to use an outside countertrade intermediary or keep the management of the transaction in-house. Assistance from intermediaries can be quite expensive but relieves the firm of the need to learn a new expertise. If companies carry out countertrade transactions in-house, the profitability of countertrade can be high. Developing in-house capability for handling countertrade, however, should be done with great caution. The table that follows provides a summary of the advantages and disadvantages of carrying out countertrade transactions within versus outsourcing them.

In-House Versus Outsourcing Countertrade Transactions

Advantages	Disadvantages
In-House	
• More profitable	• Accounting and legal expertise required
• Customer contact	• Reselling problems
• Great control	• Recruitment and training costs
• More flexibility	• Less objectivity
• More learning	• Unexpected risks and demands for countertrade
Third Parties	
• Export specialists	• May be expensive
• Customer contacts	• Distanced from customer
• Reselling contacts	• Less flexibility
• Legal and accounting expertise	• Less confidentiality
• More objectivity	• Less learning

Regardless of the decision to proceed in-house or outsource countertrade transactions, the sequence of decision making is generally the same. First, the company needs to determine the import priorities of its products to the country or firm to which it is trying to sell. Goods that are highly desirable and necessary for a country mandating countertrade are less likely to be subject to countertrade requirements than imports of goods considered luxurious and unnecessary. As a next step, the company needs to incorporate possible countertrade cost into the pricing scheme. It is quite difficult to increase the price of goods once a "cash-deal" price has been quoted and a subsequent countertrade demand is presented. At this stage, the most favored countertrade arrangement from the buyer's perspective should be identified. To do this, the company needs to determine the goals and objectives of the countertrading parties. As already discussed, these can consist of import substitution, a preservation of hard currency, export promotion, and so on.

The next step is to match the strengths of the firm with current and potential countertrade situations. The company should explore whether any internal sourcing needs can be used to fulfill a countertrade contract. This may mean that raw materials or intermediate products currently sourced from other suppliers could now be obtained from the countertrade partner. This assessment, however, should not be restricted to the internal corporate use of a countertraded product. The company should also determine whether it can use, for example, its distribution capabilities or its contacts with other customers and suppliers to help in its countertrade transactions. Moreover, an increase in the use of mandated countertrade by governments, combined with a more proactive approach toward such transactions by firms, may well result in companies expecting their suppliers to share in the burdensome effects of countertrade. At this point, the company can decide whether it should engage in countertrade transactions. The accounting and taxation aspects of the countertrade transactions should be considered, because they can often be quite different from current procedures. The use of an accounting or tax professional is essential to comply with difficult and obscure tax regulations in this area.

Next, all of the risks involved in countertrade must be assessed. This means that the goods to be obtained need to be specified, the delivery time for these goods needs to be determined, and the reliability of the supplier and the quality and consistency of the goods need to be assessed. It is also useful to explore the impact of countertrade on future prices, both for the price of the specific goods obtained and for the world market price of the category of goods. For example, a countertrade transaction may appear to be quite profitable at the time of agreement. Because months or even years may pass before the transaction is actually consummated, however, a change in world market prices may severely affect the profitability. The effect of a countertrade transaction on the world market price should also be considered. In cases of large-volume transactions, the established price may be affected, owing to a glut of supply. Such a situation not only may affect the profitability of a transaction but also can result in possible legal actions by other suppliers of similar products who feel injured by the price effects.

When evaluating the countertraded products, it is useful to determine the impact of the countertraded products on the sales and profits of other complementary product lines currently marketed by the firm. What repercussions, if any, will come about from outside groups? Such repercussions may consist of antidumping actions brought by competitors or reactions from totally unsuspected quarters. For example, McDonnell Douglas ran into strong opposition when it bartered an airplane for ham used in its employee cafeteria and as Christmas gifts. The local meat-packers' union complained vociferously that McDonnell Douglas was threatening the jobs of its members and went on strike.

Using all of the information obtained, the company can finally evaluate the length of the intended relationship with the countertrading partner and the importance of this relationship for future plans and goals. These parameters will be decisive for the final action because they may form constraints overriding short-term economic effects. Overall, management needs to remember that in most instances, a countertrade transaction should remain a means for successful international marketing and not become an end in itself.

APPENDIX

A. Terms of Sale

Incoterms and Price Quotations

Language is a fundamental part of international trade transactions. Both the buyer and seller must be aware of the intentions, desires, and instructions of the other party. Unlike national languages, international trade transactions require a common form of language whose terms and definitions are familiar to all, regardless of national language. This common language prevents misunderstandings, disputes, and miscommunication during transactions owing to different national trading practices and national language barriers.

In 1936, the International Chamber of Commerce (ICC) adopted a set of international rules, known as Incoterms, which define and interpret the concepts and instructions common to all international trade transactions. Incoterms have become accepted throughout the trading community, evolving along the way to account for new trading circumstances.

Incoterms 2000, the latest revision, became effective on January 1, 2000. In this latest version, a few terms have been streamlined and improved, notably FCA. There are 13 Incoterms. The format for Incoterms has remained unchanged. Incoterms are still ordered by Letter Group, based upon the term's first letter, and obligations are categorized by the anticipated destination of the merchandise. This method of classification is shown in the following table:

Incoterms 2000

Group E Departure	EXW	Ex Works
Group F Main Carriage Unpaid	FCA	Free Carrier
	FAS	Free Alongside Ship
	FOB	Free On Board
Group C Main Carriage Paid	CFR	Cost and Freight
	CIF	Cost, Insurance, and Freight
	CPT	Carriage, Paid to
	CIP	Carriage & Insurance Paid To
Group D Arrival	DAF	Delivered At Frontier
	DES	Delivered Ex Ship
	DEQ	Delivered Ex Quay
	DDU	Delivered Duty Unpaid
	DDP	Delivered Duty Paid

In addition to providing a standard set of terms for international trade, Incoterms play a fundamental role in the preliminary stages of a transaction. In setting up a transaction, both the buyer and seller want to maximize their interests by negotiating for contract terms most beneficial to them. This process involves negotiation over the merchandises' points of departure, form of shipping (via air or sea), costs of insurance, and delivery destination. Incoterms represent a limited form of contract between the buyer and seller to define the duties and liabilities of each party, including the transfer of risk and passage of title over the merchandise. Both the buyer and seller must be aware of how this may affect both them and the possible outcome of their transaction, including final costs, risk exposure, and profits.

E Group: Departure

Seller makes the goods available to the buyer only at the seller's own premises.

EXW (Ex Works) (. . . named place)

Ex Works is the price of the merchandise only at the point of origin, for example, the factory or manufacturing plant. The buyer or importer pays for all costs of loading the merchandise from the factory, clearing the goods for export through, and shipping it to the chosen destination. The seller has no responsibility for the merchandise once it leaves the factory.

All export licenses and documentation are the responsibility of the buyer. Only if the buyer requests assistance from the seller does the seller have any responsibility for export documentation and paperwork. Under Ex Works, the buyer is the exporter of record.

F Group: Main Carriage Unpaid

Seller is called upon to deliver the goods to a carrier appointed by the buyer.

FCA (Free Carrier) (. . . named place)

Free Carrier is an improved term. It can be used for many varieties of transportation. Free Carrier requires the seller to provide the merchandise, pack it for shipment, and clear it for export to the care of a named carrier at a named location agreed to by both parties. This term includes all modes of transport on land and by air but does not cover water transport in the traditional sense ("over the rail"), which is still covered by the term FOB. If the buyer selects freight forwarder as the named carrier, then the seller's responsibility for the merchandise ends when it is in the forwarder's custody. Because the buyer is responsible for arranging carriage of the merchandise, FCA is a specific term requiring the seller to meet the buyer's needs for shipping the merchandise, incorporating the variety of modes of transport necessary for the seller to comply.

FAS (Free Alongside Ship) (. . . named port of shipment)

With FAS, the seller provides the merchandise alongside the vessel to be used for its shipment, including all transportation charges for getting the goods to the pier. This makes the buyer, or the selected carrier, liable for clearing the goods for export and loading them onto the ship. The seller's responsibility for the goods ends when he/she obtains a receipt of acceptance from the dock.

FOB (Free On Board) (. . . named port of shipment)

Free On Board is a step beyond FAS in that the seller delivers the merchandise to the buyer or named carrier on board the ship at the point of departure. Historically, the ship's rail signifies the point where title over the merchandise shifts from the seller to the buyer or the carrier. For sellers, FOB requires them to assume the costs of shipping the merchandise to the point of departure, packing the merchandise for container shipment (if necessary), clearing the goods through customs, paying any dock fees, and loading the goods aboard ship. It is implied that FOB requires the seller to cover all costs associated with transporting, packing, containerization, customs, and loading the merchandise on board.

Free On Board is the most preferred way of arranging trade transactions, owing to its practical nature. An ocean bill of lading is a more serviceable instrument for verifying the merchandise and compliance with the terms of transaction. Often, financial institutions suggest using FOB arrangements to discourage the use of other more time-consuming and less-verifiable arrangements.

One variation of FOB has become common when exporting from the United States. Free On Board (any U.S. port) is identical to FOB, save that it allows greater flexibility for the buyer, who is unaware of the nearest port to the point of origin, and for the seller, who wants to use the fastest and cheapest route to a port for departure.

C Group: Main Carriage Paid

Seller has to contract for carriage but without assuming the risk of loss or damage to the goods or additional costs after the dispatch.

CFR (Cost and Freight) (. . . named port of shipment)
The seller is required to pay all costs and freight charges to bring the goods to a named point of departure, on board the ship named by the buyer. Similar to FOB with respect to covering only water transport, CFR covers any additional charges necessary to obtain a clean bill of lading for the buyer. Also similar to FOB, the responsibility for the merchandise shifts from the seller to the buyer once the goods cross the ship's rail, although CFR is considered to be more of a shipping contract, whereas FOB is a delivery contract. The most important difference between the FOB and CFR is that the latter gives the seller responsibility for costs of shipping while making the buyer responsible for the risks of transit. By contrast, the seller using FOB is responsible only for the cost and risk up to the point where the buyer assumes ownership over the merchandise, once the merchandise crosses the ship's rails.

This distinction is an important characteristic of the C and F groups. The F group divides the responsibility for shipping and liability equally between the buyer and seller, which transfers with the ownership of the merchandise. The C group, however, requires the seller to bear the costs of shipping, whereas the buyer is responsible for any losses or damage to the merchandise. Once the seller delivers the merchandise to a carrier (by air or land) or the merchandise passes over a ship's rails for sea shipments, the buyer assumes the risk from international or commercial sources. The seller merely covers the costs of shipment and/or insurance without assuming the risk beyond his/her obligation to deliver the merchandise for transit. In addition, the costs of freight assumed by the seller normally include the costs to discharge the goods once they have arrived at the country of destination. Adding distinctions about the costs of discharge and any responsibilities therein should not be associated with the C group because they involve issues covered by the D group.

CIF (Cost, Insurance, and Freight) (. . . named port of destination)
This term requires the seller to assume all costs, freight charges, and the additional charges for minimum shipping insurance for the merchandise while in transit to a named port of destination. The insurance coverage usually involves coverage for 110 percent of the CIF value for all risks, from warehouse to warehouse. Any request by the buyer for additional insurance coverage usually is done through a separate arrangement with the seller. It is important to note that CIF covers only water transport and not shipping via air or land.

CPT (Carriage Paid To) (. . . named port of destination)

Carriage Paid To requires the seller to assume the freight costs for the merchandise to a named destination via any form of transport. The seller provides the merchandise to a carrier, who performs carriage by rail, road, sea, or air. The seller's responsibility for the goods ends upon delivery to the carrier for shipment. The seller assumes only the cost of shipping and not the liability.

CIP (Carriage and Insurance Paid To) (. . . named place of destination)

Carriage and Insurance Paid To requires the seller to assume responsibilities similar to CPT, except that the seller must assume the additional cost of insurance for the goods while in transit. The terms of this insurance are similar to those under CIF.

D Group: Arrival

Seller has to bear all costs and risks to bring the goods to the destination determined by the buyer.

DAF (Delivered at Frontier)

Under DAF, the seller is required to provide the merchandise to the buyer at the frontier of the buyer's country. The seller is not responsible for clearing the goods through customs, but must assume any risk involving transit of the goods. This term is seldom used and is applied only for shipments via rail or road.

DES (Delivered Ex Ship)

This requires the seller to deliver the merchandise to the seller's country and provide the goods unloaded alongside the ship. The seller is not responsible for clearing the goods through customs but must assume any risk involving transit. This is an uncommon term, which applies only to water transport.

DEQ (Delivered Ex Quay)

Similar to DES, DEQ requires the seller to deliver the merchandise via water transport to the buyer's country. The seller must bear the additional costs of clearing the goods through customs and if any costs are incurred during the process. An important aspect of this process is that the seller retains all liability and risk throughout the transit process; this shifts to the buyer only after he/she assumes title of the goods from the quay at the country of destination.

DDU (Delivered Duty Unpaid)

The seller is required to provide the merchandise to the buyer at a named destination within the buyer's country. This primarily includes the seller covering all inland transportation charges within the buyer's country. The buyer, however, must assume any customs charges or duty on the merchandise. This term is most frequently used when shipping goods through a country that maintains less stringent importation requirements, such as the European Union. Should problems with customs arise, the buyer must bear the responsibilities and any costs required to clear the goods for import. As a result, DDU is not recommended to use in countries where difficulties may arise in clearing the goods for import.

DDP (Delivered Duty Paid)

This is identical the DDU, except that the seller is responsible for all freight charges, inland transportation costs, customs charges, and risk exposure during transit. The buyer bears no costs or risk exposure, whereas the seller delivers the merchandise to a named location within the buyer's country and assumes all costs and liabilities.

B. Freight Forwarding

Freight forwarding is offered by companies that specialize in the logistical area of preparing and transporting goods that are destined for the export market. These companies will also get involved in domestic shipment. Most freight forwarders (FFs) are also integrated customs brokers, a specialized area of helping importers through the customs clearance process after goods arrive at a port or airport in their country. Freight forwarders and customs brokers in the United States are regulated by the U.S. Maritime Commission.

Freight forwarders offer an array of services, the most common of which are in the following list. All of these are key areas for the exporter to consider, with one exception. Freight forwarders are logistics specialists and should be used for their expertise in this area; however, in the last 20 years or so, most FFs have been offering document preparation and handling services to exporters that use LCs. The proposed benefit of this service is that the FF can be a one-stop-shop in coordinating the export shipment and getting all required documents to the advising/paying bank in a timely fashion. Experience suggests this benefit often doesn't occur in reality. Frequently, the FF is a bottleneck impeding prompt delivery of documents to the banks. This causes many discrepancies for late presentation. It is the seller who suffers because of this poor performance. As a result, specialized "document preparation" companies have flourished in recent years. These companies specialize in document preparation and coordinate all LC documents among the seller, FF, and the banks to assure LC compliance.

> Preshipment
> > Packaging
> > Freight quotes
> > Import documentation requirements
> > Export documentation
> Shipment
> > Transportation
> > Document handling
> Postshipment
> > Tracking
> > Arrival handling

C. Drafts and Acceptances

Drafts

Drafts are a form of common commercial currency used in international trade transactions. By definition, a draft is a negotiable financial instrument created by a bank or similar financial institution or by a seller requesting an unconditional payment in writing from one entity to another. To be used in transactions, a draft must have a signature and date from the originator/drawer. Once presented to the addressed recipient, the addressee is required to make a payment for the draft amount to either the draft's bearer or a named person on the draft.

The major parts of a draft are:

- A sum of money in figures.
- The date of issuance.
- The date when the draft is due and payable. If the draft is not to be paid immediately, it is considered a time draft payable at some future date.
- The payee is the specified person/entity to whom payment is made. The term "bearer" may be substituted, permitting the holder of the draft to receive payment.
- The drawee is the person who is responsible for paying when the draft is due.
- The drawer is the person requesting payment and owed money.

Draft Parties

There are three main parties to a draft:

- The **drawer** is the seller or exporter who requests a draft from his/her bank for a trade transaction or prepares the draft himself/herself.
- The **drawee** is the entity to whom the draft is addressed. This may be a buyer, importer, or a bank fulfilling a letter of credit (LC) transaction.
- The **payee** is the person to whom payment is directed. In an LC transaction, this person is also known as the beneficiary.

The eight points of negotiability in a draft are:

- Date
- Currency value in numbers
- Currency value in words
- Payee = name of beneficiary
- Drawee = name and address of obligor
- Signer and name of beneficiary
- Specific due date
- Proper endorsement

Draft Process

Drafts provide the parties in an international trade transaction with a form of security because they are negotiable financial instruments. Consequently, there is a common factor in two payment procedures, documentary collection and LC. The steps in an LC are listed in the following:

- The beneficiary requests a draft from the bank or prepares one himself/herself to cover the costs of a buyer's ordered merchandise.
- Made out to the drawee bank, the draft accompanies the commercial documents when they are submitted to the drawee/paying bank for payment.
- Once compliance is verified by the drawee/paying bank, this bank begins the payment process with the seller.
- Once the draft is endorsed, the payment is sent to the remitting bank.

The steps in a documentary collection are listed in the following:

- The seller prepares his/her own draft or uses his/her bank's documentary collection form that automatically includes a draft to cover the total value of the product.

- Made out to the buyer as the drawee, the draft is sent with the commercial documents to the collecting bank in the buyer's country.
- The collecting bank notifies the buyer about the documents and releases the documents to the buyer when it receives funds from the buyer.
- Once the draft is endorsed by the buyer, the payment is sent to the remitting bank.

Because a draft is negotiable, the endorsement and draft presentation are flexible, to meet the requirements of the parties in a transaction. The draft presentation may require the paying bank to submit payment to the beneficiary immediately if it is a sight draft; however, this payment can be delayed until a specific future date if a time or usance draft is employed. If desired by the parties, the draft may require a special endorsement in order to authorize payment to the beneficiary. The types of endorsements are as follows:

- If a draft can be endorsed in *blank,* the buyer passes title over the document to whoever is bearer of the paper, allowing immediate payment upon presentation. When the endorser simply writes his/her name on the back of the draft, the draft is said to have been endorsed in blank. Even though a blank endorsed draft is bearer paper, the holder may make it payable specifically to himself/herself by writing immediately above the blank endorsement the phrase "Pay to the order of (the holder's name)."
- With a *special endorsement,* also called a restricted endorsement, the bearer of the draft must have the signature of a specified endorsee before the draft can be negotiated. This restricts negotiating over a draft to the specified endorsee. Once the restricted endorsee has endorsed the draft, it is available for further negotiation/endorsement. Each subsequent endorsee has full recourse to all prior endorsees in the event of a failure to pay the draft's amount. In addition, a person/entity holding a specially endorsed draft in its name is protected against loss or theft of the draft prior to its endorsement. The subsequent finder of the draft cannot negotiate it without the missing endorsement of the holder. If the finder supplies the missing endorsement, the finder commits fraud. Most endorsements on drafts are of this type.
- If the endorsee selects to limit his/her liability for a draft, he/she gives it a *qualified endorsement.* This limits the endorsee's liability for the draft, should it pass to another endorser and not be honored. This type of endorsement is most commonly recognized by the words "without

recourse" being added to the endorsement. Banks will not purchase/ discount a draft so endorsed, because the endorser is effectively saying that no one has recourse to him/her if the draft is not paid. The qualified endorser, however, does not lose his/her rights to look to all other endorsers prior to its endorsement in the event of default.

Acceptances

In international trade transactions, the use of time drafts is common when the parties choose to delay payment on a transaction until a future, determined date. This time draft is also known as an *acceptance,* because when paying/drawee banks in LCs or buyers/drawees in documentary collections commit themselves to pay at a future date, they mark the draft as "Accepted" by signing the face of the draft. This signifies that the draft, now called an acceptance, may be executed on the date specified as the maturity date.

Trade acceptances are time drafts drawn as part of documentary collections and refer to the "documents against acceptance" payment procedure. The exporter draws a time draft and expects the buyer to accept it in return for documents permitting the receipt of shipped merchandise. If accepted by the buyer, the acceptance becomes a trade acceptance, owing to its association with the shipment of merchandise.

Banker's Acceptances

Should a seller have any doubts concerning the willingness of the buyer to make payment on an acceptance at the time of maturity, then a banker's acceptance is an alternative financial instrument providing more certainty of payment. A banker's acceptance is a time draft similar to other acceptances, except that the paying bank accepts the draft as the drawee, legally committing itself to honor payment of the draft at maturity. On the maturity date, the paying bank makes payment, eliminating any concern about nonpayment on the seller's part. Having this guarantee of payment is useful for the seller, who may either keep the banker's acceptance until maturity or request the bank to discount the draft. By discounting the draft, the bank gives the seller the draft's face value less a percentage based on the number of days until maturity and the bank's discount rate. Because this rate is often the lowest interest rate available, discounting is an advantageous form of financing. In addition to reducing the draft's value, banks may also charge an acceptance fee for processing the draft.

Some clarification about the types of banker's acceptances is necessary with regard to the payment procedure employed in a transaction. A *documentary banker's acceptance* deals with LC transactions or documentary collections. These require submitting necessary commercial documents associated with the terms of an LC or documentary collection. By contrast, a *clean banker's acceptance* deals with transactions not requiring the presentation of commercial documents to validate compliance with a transaction's terms, such as in open account transactions.

Eligibility is an important factor in using banker's acceptances because it may affect an exporter's attempts to discount the acceptance. The U.S. Federal Reserve has established criteria for determining whether banker's acceptances are eligible or ineligible for discounting. The criteria for banker's acceptances to be eligible for discounting are:

- the acceptance's term cannot exceed six months from the date of acceptance to the time of maturity;
- the date of acceptance must be within a reasonable time period from the date of shipment of the merchandise, usually 30 days;
- the trade transaction must be self-liquidating, requiring the transaction to produce funds capable of paying off the acceptance and matching the tenor of the acceptance with the time period required to complete the transaction; and
- the trade transactions must involve the import or export of goods between the United States and another country, the domestic shipment of goods within the United States, and/or the storage of marketable staples in a warehouse in the United States or another country.

Should an acceptance not meet these requirements, the Federal Reserve requires the paying bank to maintain a reserve with regard to making payment. In effect, this may raise the cost of discounting an acceptance by 30 percent to 50 percent. Even with the additional costs, financing with banker's acceptances may be less expensive than alternative means of financing.

Financing with Trade/Banker's Acceptances

Holding a trade acceptance, a seller may be able to obtain financing for a trade transaction by using the acceptance as collateral. The seller may offer the acceptance to a bank at a discount, which gives the acceptance's holder its face value minus a discount based upon the number of days to maturity and the bank's discount rate. The bank may or may not have recourse to the drawee, depending upon the nature of the acceptance.

The seller may also seek a loan using the trade acceptance as collateral. Typically, the seller can obtain 60 percent to 80 percent of the acceptance's face value, with the proceeds of the acceptance's maturity value going toward paying the loan plus any interest. The bank providing the loan usually retains full recourse against the seller unless they agree to rely on the acceptance as their collateral. The seller may also use a trade acceptance as collateral to obtain a banker's acceptance, although this option is more difficult to obtain from U.S. banks.

Banker's Acceptance Financing

In a trade transaction, both buyers and sellers may obtain financing separate from the terms of a transaction by using a bankers' acceptance. Should buyers need financing prior to the arrival of ordered merchandise, they may apply for a time draft from their bank. Upon determining eligibility, the bank can discount the draft and provide the funds immediately to the seller. The discount and any fees are paid by the buyer at maturity of the acceptance. Using this type of financing, the buyer does not have to make payment on the time draft until the maturity date. This extends low-rate financing for the buyer while giving the seller funds immediately.

When a bank discounts an acceptance, it reduces its face value based upon the bank's *all-in-rate*. This rate is the combination of the discount interest rates available in the market and the bank's own acceptance fee, which typically is about 1.5 percent per annum. The discount rate is usually slightly below LIBOR and the American prime rate. It varies according to market conditions and the characteristics of the acceptance (the accepting bank, the date of maturity, and so forth); the all-in-rate is the amount quoted to the person seeking a discount. Banks use an *effective rate* to determine the actual cost to the bank for discounting an acceptance. This is higher than the all-in-rate and should be the major consideration when comparing discounting rates among several banks. When discounting, banks deduct all interest due at the time of the borrowing. Banks may rediscount an acceptance by selling it to a dealer or any willing investor. Banker's acceptances are often attractive investments and banks are willing to rediscount an acceptance in order to obtain "matching" funds so as not to reduce the bank's available funds and increase its own liquidity.

There are many advantages and disadvantages to financing with banker's acceptances. On the advantageous side:

- It allows an exporter to obtain immediate funds while permitting the buyer extended payment terms.
- It offers advantageous terms, which are better than most market terms.
- The repayment process corresponds with the cash flow needs of the buyer in the trade transaction.

On the negative side, banker's acceptance financing:

- is strictly short-term, with financing terms only up to six months.
- is restricted to the requirements established by the U.S. Federal Reserve.

Alternative financing is also available should a seller's only recourse be using an ineligible banker's acceptance. Discounting ineligible banker's acceptances is a possible means of obtaining financing. Federal Reserve requirements state that the discounting bank must maintain a reserve account to insure payment on the acceptance at maturity, resulting in a higher discount rate than for an eligible banker's acceptance.

D. Commercial Documents

Shipper's Export Declaration (SED)

The *Shipper's Export Declaration (SED)* is a government-required document stating the type of export license used to determine if the merchandise is authorized for export. This document is required for all exports with a value greater than $2,500. Included in this form are the proper Schedule B Number, the quantities of merchandise to be shipped, the FOB value of the shipment, and the final destination.

Commercial Invoice

A *commercial invoice* is a record of all transactions between a buyer and seller, including all terms, conditions, and modes of transport involved in the transaction. It is important to include such specific information as:

- the order date and number;
- shipping date;
- method of shipment;
- terms of sale;
- payment terms;
- a description of the merchandise;
- unit and total price; and
- the total shipping charges.

For LC transactions, the invoice should include:

- the letter's number or any other financial documents such as drafts, acceptances, and fees involved in the transactions;
- a reference to a shipping-invoice document, whether an air waybill for air transport or an ocean bill of lading; and
- all necessary transit information.

The purpose of a commercial invoice is to provide a concise record of a transaction both for the parties of a transaction but also for any government or customs officials. Also, the LC verification procedures will require detailed information on the transaction to ensure compliance with the credit's terms. Consequently, a commercial invoice should be error-free and have the proper signatures and legal statement signifying authenticity. Such as statement might read as follows:

"We certify the above merchandise is in accordance with buyer's order, that it is of (country involved) origin and manufacture, and that the invoice is true and correct in all particulars."

Consular Invoices

Consular invoices are often required in many countries for customs or documentary reasons. They must contain information similar to a commercial invoice and have the same attention to detail.

Packing List

A *packing list* is a common requirement for clearing merchandise through a country's customs procedures. It should include a complete listing of all merchandise in a shipment, including the type, package materials, dimensions, unit value, and physical location within a transit container or cargo hold. It should include shipping marks with the port destination and the buyer's and seller's reference numbers.

It is important that the list be legal and error-free, like the commercial invoice, with official signatures. A copy of the list should be attached to the first carton of the merchandise to be shipped.

Certificate of Origin

A *certificate of origin* declares that the goods being shipped originate in a particular country. This must be broken down to include other countries if the merchandise comes from several countries. In addition, the certificate must be of legal quality and countersigned by a local chamber of commerce. Some countries require certificates to have a visa from the resident consul of the specified country.

Insurance Certificate

The *insurance certificate* is proof that the shipment is insured.

- The certificate must state the details of the shipment, including the destination, merchandise, and point of origin.

- It must list the policy's date of coverage, which must at least be by the time of loading on board for transit.
- It should provide the risks covered by the policy; that the currency stated in the policy and in the LC are the same; and that the policy will cover at least 115 percent of the CIF value.

Ocean Bill of Lading

An *ocean bill of lading* is the contract between the shipper and the carrier to ship the merchandise. This is a negotiable document, allowing the owner of the merchandise in the carrier's custody to transfer title over the goods to another person. It includes a complete listing of the goods loaded on board, complete with merchandise and packing details, and the name of the person to receive the goods and assume title at the destination. Because an ocean bill of lading is a contract, it is subject to the provisions of the U.S. Carriage of Goods at Sea Act, which must be detailed on the opposite side of an ocean bill of lading.

There are several different types of ocean bills of lading:

- A *straight bill of lading* is an ocean bill of lading made out to the named consignee and is generally not negotiable.
- A *negotiable bill of lading* is made out in blank and delivered to the recipient, who endorses it to receive the merchandise. This blank endorsement allows for third parties in the transaction to receive the merchandise as part of documentary collections or other similar payment procedures.
- A *bill of lading to order* is made out to the order of the shipper and endorsed, whether in blank or to a named consignee. This allows the shipper to retain control over the merchandise until payment is received, because the recipient cannot receive the merchandise until the shipper endorses the bill of lading. It is important that the bill of lading specify whether it is endorsed "in blank" or to a specific person.

There are additional characteristics regarding ocean bills of lading:

- A *clean bill of lading* indicates that there are no conditions or exceptions attached to the original bill of lading.
- A *foul bill of lading* is the opposite of a clean bill and may include notes or riders defining the condition of the merchandise as bad or damaged.
- The *original bill of lading* is the document issued by the carriage company once the vessel has left port, which includes three copies of the bill of

lading, each signed and stamped by the carriage company. The set of three copies is known collectively as the original bill of lading.

Air Waybill

An *air waybill* is similar to an ocean bill of lading, save it is restricted to shipping by airfreight. Another major difference between the two is that an air waybill is nonnegotiable. It is the contract between the shipper and the airfreight carrier, limited to the conditions stated on the waybill, such as the destination and recipient.

E. Export Assistance Programs

Bankers' Association for Foreign Trade (BAFT)

Access to Export Capital Program (AXCAP)

The Access to Export Capital Program (AXCAP), operated by the Bankers' Association for Foreign Trade (BAFT), is a national database listing of banks and government agencies involved in trade finance and the services they offer. The AXCAP matches specific exporter needs with appropriate financial services. For first-time exporters or seasoned exporters looking for new markets, AXCAP helps customize financing options for businesses in global markets. Exporters will reach a trade specialist who will pinpoint specific trade finance problems and provide the exporter with a list of banks and government agencies that offer the needed services.

Contact:
Access to Export Capital Program
Bankers' Association for Foreign Trade
2121 K Street, NW—Suite 701
Washington DC 20037
Tel: (202) 452-0013
Fax: (202) 452-0959
Internet Address: www.baft.org

Department of Defense

Defense Export Loan Guarantee (DELG) Program

The Defense Export Loan Guarantee (DELG) Program enables the Secretary of Defense to guarantee private-sector loans made to foreign sovereigns for the purchase or long-term lease of U.S. defense articles and services. The program strives to meet U.S. security objectives by encouraging interoperability of defense systems with its allies and to enable U.S. exporters to better compete in the international marketplace. The DELG program serves as a credit enhancement facility, allowing eligible foreign countries to achieve favorable borrowing terms and additional cash-flow management flexibility.

The DELG program guarantees 85 percent of contract value or 100 percent of U.S. content, whichever is lesser in value. Defense exports must have a minimum of 50 percent U.S. content. The program offers a disbursement period (interest payments only) of up to 5 years and a repayment period of up to 12 years. A cash payment of at least 15 percent of the contract value must be paid to the supplier prior to the disbursement of the guaranteed loan amount or in installments of at least 15 percent of the value of each payment.

The DELG program is similar to Ex-Im Bank's loan guarantee programs except that foreign sovereigns bear all program costs, the exposure fee may not be included in the guaranteed loan amount, and the program pertains to defense exports as defined by the Arms Export Control Act only.

Eligibility. Countries eligible for DELG assistance include NATO members, major non-NATO allies, emerging democracies of Central Europe, and non-communist members of Asian Pacific Economic Cooperation (APEC). Eligible export items are defined in the Arms Export Control Act (22 U.S.C. 2751) and described in the United States Munitions List (22 CFR, Chapter I, Part 121). Appropriate export licenses from the U.S. Department of State are required before the Department of Defense will issue a final loan guarantee (see Chapter Two). Defense Export Loan Guarantee Program guarantees may be applied to both direct commercial sales as well as sales made through the United States Foreign Military Sales program.

Contact:
Defense Export Loan Guarantee Program
Office of the Deputy Undersecretary of Defense
The Pentagon—Room 3E1082
Washington DC 20301-3070
Tel: (703) 697-2685
Fax: (703) 695-5343
Internet address: www.delg.org

F. United Nations Convention on the International Sale of Goods

The goal of the United Nations Convention on the International Sale of Goods (CISG) was to harmonize the rules regarding the international sale of goods. It was created in 1980 by the United Nations Commission on International Trade Law (UNCITRAL). The United States ratified the CISG and it entered into force on January 1, 1988. As of May 1992, the CISG has been ratified by over 30 countries including China, Canada, Mexico, Germany, France, Sweden, Italy, and Russia.

The clearest statement of purpose for the CISG is provided in Article 4, which states that the "Convention governs only the formation of the contract of sale and the rights and obligations of the seller and the buyer arising from such a contract." This includes issues of offer, acceptance, and obligations of the buyer and seller. Moreover, the scope of the CISG is limited to contracts for the international commercial sale of goods.

The CISG does not apply to certain issues which arise in contracts, such as validity of a contract, including fraud in the inducement, authority or capacity to enter a contract, whether a contract violates domestic law, and what rights a third party might have in property sold under this contract. Moreover, issues of products liability are not covered in the CISG.

Similar to the Uniform Commercial Code (UCC), the CISG is designed to have any gaps filled "in conformity with the general principles on which it (the CISG) is based." They both rely on some of the same broad concepts of contract law such as trade usages and good faith. The following, however, are the most important distinctions between CISG and the UCC that might have an impact on an international transaction:

- Under the CISG, a sales contract may fail owing to indefiniteness if the price or some provision for determining price is not supplied. By contrast, the UCC allows a contract to be formed even without a sales price.
- Under the CISG, an offer becomes irrevocable upon reliance. Under the UCC, an irrevocable offer must be in writing.
- The "mailbox rule" is different under the CISG. Under the CISG, acceptance occurs upon receipt. Under prevailing U.S. law, the acceptance occurs when it is placed in the mailbox.
- The "battle of the forms" is handled differently. If an acceptance is returned with changes in the terms of the offer, the CISG deems this to be a rejection of the offer and the modification is viewed as a counteroffer. This view gives practical effect to the "mirror image

rule." Under the UCC, a contract is deemed to have been formed even if the acceptance is not on the exact same terms as the offer.

- Finally, the CISG does not require that a sales contract be in writing. Rather, the CISG takes the view that the contract's existence can be proven by other means. Yet, the UCC provides that many contracts must be in writing.

The Use of CISG in the Drafting of Agreements

The CISG will apply automatically to international sales contracts between buyers and sellers located in countries that have ratified the CISG. It can be incorporated into an agreement by reference even if the parties to the agreement are not from countries that have ratified and enacted the CISG. Similarly, the parties can opt out of the CISG or one or more provisions of the CISG by mutual consent, even if both parties are from countries that have ratified the CISG. The greatest single benefit of using the CISG is the certainty that is introduced by using an established and accepted regime.

It is important to ensure that the international sales agreement has adequate provisions for resolving disputes under the agreement. In addition to the "traditional" terms that exist in both domestic and international sales agreements, unique provisions must be added often or traditional provisions must be modified when sales contracts are dealt with in the international market. For example:

- A *language* of the contract must be selected and the text in that language must be clearly designated as the definitive and official version of the agreement.
- The *choice of law* provision, which exists in domestic contracts, takes on new significance because of the vast differences in legal regimes that could be applied to an international contract. The law that might be applied to a contract in a Middle Eastern country could be very different from the law that might be applied in a western legal system.
- The *dispute settlement* provision must be carefully drafted.

The international sales agreement will contain many of the same provisions any domestic agreement would, that is, risk of loss and allocation of transportation and insurance costs. Price and delivery terms should be established by using International Commercial Terms (INCOTERMS). The price or method for determining the price must be stated clearly; as was noted previously, this may be critical under the CISG. One should also be careful to assure that the sales transaction is not viewed as a licensing of an intellectual property right.

Agency and Distributor Agreements

Agents

In general, agents do not buy and sell for their own account. Rather, they receive commission on sales they make on behalf of companies they represent, the principals. Because agents do not own the products they sell, the risk of loss remains with the company the agent represents. Furthermore, agents may or may not have the power to accept orders, obligate the principal, or set sales price or sales terms.

It is also important to remember that civil code and common law countries treat the agency relationship very differently. For example, the liability of a principal for the acts of undisclosed agents is a concept unique to the common law countries. In addition, it is important to remember that there may be other local laws that will affect the principal/agent relationship. For example, there may requirements of local representation. That is, local laws may require that any sales made to a party within the country must employ local sales agents, who are nationals of that country. This type of requirement is found in many Middle Eastern countries.

Moreover, some countries do not allow certain types of sales through agents. Other countries may require contracts with local agents to be registered and certain information be disclosed (that is, the amount of the commission). Some countries have limitations on the amount of commissions that may be paid to local agents and require that the agreements be exclusive. Finally, there may also be restrictions on the termination of agency agreements.

Distributors

Distributors are different from agents. They generally make a larger financial commitment to a market and often receive exclusive rights to sell for this commitment. The key legal distinctions between an agent and distributor are:

- A distributor takes title to the goods and, therefore, accepts the risk of loss and makes profits by reselling the goods.
- Distributors cannot contractually bind the company producing the goods.
- Distributors establish the price and sales terms of the goods.

Distributors do not have employment conditions subject to local labor laws; however, the distributor could be protected by other statutes and, therefore, one should include a "no employment relationship" provision in the agreement.

Drafting Considerations for Agency and Distributor Agreements
The first and most important consideration is to ensure that the agreement clearly states what the relationship actually is—agent or distributor. As discussed in the preceding sections, the rights and duties of the two different relationships are very significant. Given this distinction, the agreements should state very plainly and clearly what relationship is being established.

The agreements should also clarify the terms and conditions for selling the products, for example:

- Determine whether the relationship is exclusive versus non-exclusive.
- State which geographic regions are to be covered.
- Set forth issues of payment for the products (in the case of a distributor) and for payments of commissions (in the case of agents).
- Determine the currency in which payments are to be made and address currency fluctuation issues.
- Provide specific provisions regarding renewal of the agreement, including specific parameters for performance, promotional activity, and notice of desire to renew.
- Establish a specific provision for termination of the agreement and for what reasons, that is, failure to perform to the terms of the contract. (Be careful with this provision. Some foreign countries restrict or prohibit termination without just cause or compensation.)
- Outline the termination process for the end of the agreement period.
- Provide for workable and acceptable dispute settlement clauses.
- Assure that the agreement addresses whether intellectual property rights are being licensed or reserved.
- Prevent, unless with seller consent, the contract to be assigned to another party (subagents or subdistributors) to be used to fulfill obligations in the contract or the contract to be transferred with a change of ownership or control over the agent/distributor.
- Assure that your contract complies with both U.S. and foreign laws on topics such as export and import licenses; customs duties and sales taxes; relevant antitrust/competition laws relating to marketing restrictions and pricing methods; and relevant laws on bribery (Foreign Corrupt Practices Act) and employment and marketing discrimination (Anti-Boycott Law).

G. Microfinance

As an exporter, are you finding potential buyers who want your products and could use them productively to generate sufficient cash flow to pay for them, but for some reason they are unable to arrange financing for the transaction?

Does your marketing research indicate a large unmet demand for your products, yet you are having difficulty reaching them because of their lack of credit history, collateral, or access to commercial credit? Are you finding that selling to well-connected importers is unprofitable, although they are able to yield high returns by reselling your products locally for several times the price without adding any value? If the answer to any of these questions is yes, microfinance may have some valuable insights for you to consider that may dramatically alter the way you reach your exporting goals.

Background

Many developing countries have large income disparities, which translates into a small but extremely wealthy upper class, a slightly larger middle class, and a vast lower class. Traditionally, the middle- and upper classes have had access to the financial system, whereas the lower class has been excluded. Experience has shown that in many cases, the lower class has been marginalized because of rigid credit procedures, standardized products that do not meet their needs, and a general unwillingness by commercial banks to view them as a viable client base. As a result, most low-income individuals have been forced to use informal financing mechanisms, such as moneylenders and pawnbrokers who can charge over 3,000 percent per year.[23] Therefore, skilled but poor entrepreneurs who have no access to institutional credit can be trapped firmly in a system of debt, poverty, and exploitation.

Seeing the great need for a catalyst in economic development, a number of microfinance institutions (MFIs) have been established worldwide to provide loans, savings, and other basic financial services to the poor. Their vision is that people living in poverty, like everyone else, need a diverse range of financial instruments to run their businesses, build assets, stabilize consumption, and shield themselves against risks. These MFIs aimed to provide the following specific financial services to the poor: working capital loans, consumer credit, savings, pensions, insurance, and money transfer services.[24]

One of the foremost MFIs in the world is Grameen Bank, a nongovernmental, self-funded organization with origins in Bangladesh.[25] By providing loans that range from $35 and averaging $100 to "the poorest of the poor," Grameen became necessarily women-focused: 96 percent of its customers are

---

[23] *Grameen: Banking for the Poor.* 20 July 2005. Accessed from www.grameen-info.org in July 2005.

[24] "Key Principles of Microfinance—CGAP". Consultative Group to Assist the Poor. 2003. Accessed from www.cgap.org in July 2005.

[25] Section adapted from Nguyen, Sabrina. *Banking on the World's Poor: Microfinancing and the Fight Against Poverty.* April 2005. Georgetown University, McDonough School of Business.

female.[26] By design, Grameen's ownership and control remain in the hands of the very people to whom it lends. As soon as a borrower accumulates sufficient saving, she buys one—and only one—$3-share in Grameen. The Bank's interest rate is set such that after-tax profits cover only operational expenses and any residuals are returned to shareholder-borrowers in the form of dividends. Since its inception in 1983, Grameen has provided over $1 billion in loans to over 3 million borrowers, and its model has been adapted in more than 100 countries spanning five continents.[27] With on-time loan repayments of 98 percent and defaults at less than 0.05 percent, Grameen's clients have shattered the notion that the poor are bad credit risks and proved that given affordable capital, they could and would improve their lives.[28]

The Role of Microfinance in Exporting

How does all of this relate to your business activities? Because low-income individuals represent the vast majority of the population in developing countries and have very little financial capital, there is enormous market potential if productive capital investments are provided. In short, both the poor as buyers and you as a seller stand to benefit from the exchange. The challenge, however, is to enable the poor to amass the initial sum of capital needed to purchase your product in order to begin increasing their earning potential. This is where microfinance can play an important role.

Thousands of MFIs worldwide have developed revolutionary credit and savings technologies that have increased the poor's access to formal banking services. In one way or another, these institutions have found successful means of leveraging the poor's need for a reliable source of affordable credit and their nontraditional assets, such as social standing within a group or community, to create the incentives for on-time loan repayment. As a result, a significant portion of these institutions has become sustainable and profitable over time.

The implications for you, as an exporter, is that many MFIs are ready and willing to provide your potential clients the credit they need to buy your products. The first task is to locate the MFIs, recruit their efforts, and educate potential clients about the services available to them.

Although the relative newness of microfinance makes it difficult to find information on MFIs, there are several reputable services available to the

---

[26] *Grameen: Banking for the Poor.* 20 July 2005. Accessed from www.grameen-info.org in July 2005.

[27] Yunus, Muhammad and Alan Jolis. *Banker to the Poor: The Autobiography of Muhammad Yunus, Founder of Grameen Bank.* New York, NY: Oxford University Press, 2001.

[28] Ibid.

general public that can help guide the search. For example, the Microfinance Information eXchange (MIX) is a Washington DC–based nonprofit organization whose mission is to promote the flow of information about the microfinance community to the formal financial sector and the public. One of the means by which MIX accomplishes this is through its website, the MIX Market (www.mixmarket.org). The site provides detailed information on both supply (donors/investors) and demand (MFIs) for institutional funding. It features over 359 sortable and comparable MFI financial statements and ratios, ratings reports and audits, information on MFI networks, and terms and conditions of funding from investors and donors. Furthermore, each institution that posts its information on the MIX Market is encouraged to disclose information in the following three categories: general information, such as mission, region of operation, contact information, and external references; outreach, which includes the number of borrowers and savers; and financial performance, including institutional ratings. Therefore, the MIX Market can be an invaluable tool to identify the location, sustainability, and viability of MFIs worldwide.

Another available search tool is the Microfinance Gateway (www.microfinancegateway.org), the largest online library on microfinance and a project of the World Bank's Consultative Group to Assist the Poor (CGAP). One of CGAP's central principals is that microfinance works best when it measures and discloses its performance. Therefore, through its Microfinance Rating and Assessment Fund, the Microfinance Gateway provides reliable and standardized financial data (for example, interest rates, loan repayment, and cost recovery) and social information (for example, number of clients reached and their poverty level) on MFIs worldwide.

As an anti-poverty movement, microfinance has proven to be a successful far-reaching strategy that is both permanent and self-sustaining. For the exporter in particular, the design of the microfinance industry itself provides immense business opportunities by providing credit to a new landscape of potential importers: Over 2,931 MFIs worldwide service over 81 million clients.[29] Therefore, it is a valuable proposition for exporters to partner with MFIs to identify possible trade relationships. This not only provides financial incentives for the exporter, but also allows individuals in less-developed countries to improve the quality of their lives by leveraging their human capital and financial capital with their entrepreneurial spirit.

---

[29] Daley-Harris, Sam. *State of the Microcredit Summit Report 2004.* Washington DC: Microfinance Summit Campaign, 2004.

OMB No.: 3420-0011
Expiration: 12/31/2007
OPIC-52

Application for
Political Risk Insurance

Overseas Private Investment Corporation
An Agency of the United States Government

1100 New York Avenue, N.W.
Washington, DC 20527
www.opic.gov

Insurance Department
Tel.: (202) 336-8400
Fax: (202) 408-5142

Application for Political Risk Insurance

The Overseas Private Investment Corporation (OPIC) requests information on this application to determine whether the Investor and the project meet eligibility requirements for insurance, specifically with regard to underwriting criteria and legislative and regulatory compliance. Information provided to OPIC must be accurate as of the date an OPIC contract is issued. Responses to questions that call for estimates or projections should take the form of good faith statements made to the best of the Investor's knowledge and belief, after due inquiry. Misrepresentations or failure to disclose relevant information may result in the cancellation of insurance. Neither issuance of a registration letter nor acknowledgment of receipt of this application implies that the investment is eligible for political risk insurance or that a contract will be issued.

The information contained in this application will be designated as privileged or confidential in accordance with the Freedom of Information Act (FOIA) regulations (22 CFR Part 706) and will be treated as confidential to the extent permitted OPIC by FOIA.

INSTRUCTIONS:

Please contact an insurance officer at (202) 336-8400 if you have any questions about this application.

1) All applicants must fill out Parts 1 through 12.

3) All applicants must provide the certifications requested in Parts 2, 9 and 10.

4) Please note in Part 11 that OPIC may require supplemental information.

5) If you use an attachment to answer any of the questions in this application, please write "see Attachment" in the appropriate answer block and indicate the corresponding question number on your attachment.

6) All applicants applying for OPIC insurance must sign this application in Part 12. If an Investor is applying for OPIC insurance on behalf of other eligible Investors, OPIC also will require the ultimate beneficiary Investors to sign this application.

7) When completed, please submit:

    (a) Completed application, and

    (b) One (1) copy of all attachments and supporting documentation.

    Mailing Address:*

    Applications Officer – Insurance Department
    Overseas Private Investment Corporation
    1100 New York Avenue, N.W.
    Washington, DC 20527

---

* Signed applications may be submitted by fax to (202) 408-5142. Alternatively, signed electronic applications (for example in Adobe PDF or other readable formats) may be submitted by electronic mail to SWILL1@opic.gov. Supporting documentation may be submitted by fax to (202) 408-5142 or by electronic mail to SWILL1@opic.gov.

BUSINESS CONFIDENTIAL INFORMATION

Part 1: Investor Information (Investor to be Insured by OPIC)

1. **Name of Investor:**

   Address:

   City: State: Zip/Postal Code:

   Country: Telephone: Fax:

   E-Mail: Web site:

2. **Type of Investor** *(check one investor type only)*
   - ☐ Entity Organized Under U.S. Law
     - (a) Is more than 50 percent of both the total equity interest and each class of equity interests issued by the Investor and outstanding on the date hereof beneficially owned by U.S. citizens?[1]
       ☐ Yes   ☐ No   *(If No, please contact OPIC before proceeding.)*
     - (b) Is this entity a minority-owned business?   (c) Is this entity a women-owned business?
       ☐ Yes   ☐ No   ☐ Yes   ☐ No
   - ☐ Individual Investor
     - (a) Is the Investor a citizen of the United States?
       ☐ Yes   ☐ No
   - ☐ Entity Organized Outside of the United States
     - (a) If organized other than as a corporation, is 100 percent of both the total equity interest and each class of shares or equity interests issued by the Investor and outstanding beneficially owned by U.S. citizens?
       ☐ Yes   ☐ No   *(If No, please contact OPIC before proceeding.)*
     - (b) If organized as a corporation, is five percent or more of any class of equity interests or shares issued by the Investor and outstanding beneficially owned by persons other than U.S. citizens?
       ☐ Yes   ☐ No   *(If Yes, please contact OPIC before proceeding.)*

3. **Name of Person OPIC should contact for information:**

   Title: Company:

   Address:

   City: State: Zip/Postal Code:

   Country: Telephone: Fax:

   E-Mail: Web site:

4. **How did you learn about OPIC and its services?**
   - ☐ conference   ☐ OPIC Web site   ☐ other government agency (SBA, TDA, EX-IM)
   - ☐ insurance broker ☐ former OPIC clients ☐ other *(please explain)*

1) OPIC deems a corporation organized under the laws of the U.S. or its states or territories to be beneficially owned by U.S citizens if more than 50 percent of each class of its issued and outstanding stock is owned by U.S. citizens either directly or beneficially.

Part 2: Private Political Risk Insurance

OPIC strongly encourages Investors to consider carefully the availability of private political risk insurance for their investments abroad. OPIC only offers insurance to Investors who, having investigated the possibility of obtaining insurance from private political risk insurers, decide to pursue OPIC insurance because private insurance is not available on terms sufficient to make the investment viable for the Investor, or because of specific benefits OPIC participation will bring to the investment. To assist us in meeting this objective, OPIC requests that applicants respond to the following questions:

5. Have you sought political risk insurance from the private market for the project?[2]

   ☐ Yes   ☐ No

   If <u>Yes</u>, is insurance available from private political risk insurers?

   ☐ Yes   ☐ No

7. In either event, please indicate at least two of the private market political risk insurers with which you have discussed this project.

   1) _____

   2) _____

8. If private political risk insurance is available, is it in the amount necessary and on terms sufficient for the project's viability?

   ☐ Yes   ☐ No

   If <u>Yes</u>, please explain why political risk insurance being sought from OPIC? If <u>No</u>, please explain.

Part 3: Project Information

9. OPIC Registration of Insurance Number: _____ *(See OPIC registration letter for assigned number.)*

10. Briefly describe the project. Please attach a copy of information memoranda, business plans, or other descriptions of the project that would be helpful to OPIC's understanding of the project.

---

2) Providers of political risk insurance in the private market include companies such as AIG, Chubb, Unistrat, Sovereign and Zurich.

BUSINESS CONFIDENTIAL INFORMATION

11. **Please specify whether this project is:**
    ☐ an expansion of an existing enterprise   ☐ a new (greenfield) enterprise
    ☐ privatization of a state-owned company   ☐ other *(please explain)* _____

12. **Where is the project located?** *(Please attach a map showing the location.)*

_____

13. **Describe any host government involvement in the project.**

14. **Name of the entity (the "Foreign Enterprise") in the host country into which the investment will be made:**

    Foreign Enterprise:

    Address:

    City: Postal Code: Country:

    Telephone: Fax: E-Mail:

15. **Please identify and describe briefly any current or past disputes with respect to this project that involve any agency or instrumentality of the host government. Include all disputes with any agency or instrumentality of the host government that have in the past involved or currently involve the Investor, the Foreign Enterprise, or any participants in the project.**

Part 4: Investor Representations

16. **Eligibility to conduct business with the United States Government**
    Is the Investor, any related party or affiliate of the Investor, or any supplier to the project currently suspended, debarred or voluntarily excluded from procurement or nonprocurement dealings with the United States Government (Executive Order 12549 February 18, 1986, 51 CFR 6370)?
    ☐ Yes   ☐ No   *If Yes, please contact OPIC before proceeding.*

17. **Foreign Corrupt Practices Act[3]**

    (a) To the best of the Investor's knowledge after due inquiry, has the Investor ever been the subject of an investigation under the Foreign Corrupt Practices Act of 1977, as amended?

    ☐ Yes   ☐ No   *If Yes, please contact OPIC before proceeding.*

    (b) Has the Investor been convicted of, or been party to a final adverse administrative determination of, an offense under the Foreign Corrupt Practices Act of 1977, as amended?

    ☐ Yes   ☐ No   *If Yes, please attach explanation.*

    (c) To the best of the Investor's knowledge after due inquiry, has the project been established (e.g., obtained licenses, approvals, permits, etc.) in compliance with all applicable laws pertaining to corrupt practices?

    ☐ Yes   ☐ No   *If No, please attach explanation.*

Part 5: Investment to be Insured by OPIC

18. **Please provide copies of any project documentation that would be helpful to OPIC's understanding of the project and the investment structure, such as company charter, joint venture documents, loan agreements, technical assistance agreements, management service agreements, lease agreements, loan guaranties, licenses or other agreements with the host government, etc. All documentation must be in English.**

19. **Investment to be Insured** (*Check all that apply*)

Type of Investment	Amount to be Insured
☐ Equity	$
☐ Leases	$
☐ Loans or Loan Guaranties	$
☐ Technical Assistance and Management Agreements	$

20. **Type of Coverage Sought** (*Check all that apply*)

☐ Expropriation   ☐ Political Violence for Assets   ☐ Stand-Alone Terrorism
☐ Inconvertibility   ☐ Political Violence for Business Income   ☐ Non-Honoring of a Sovereign Guarantee

21. **Term of Contract:** _____ years   *(OPIC can offer a minimum term of 3 years and a maximum term of 20 years)*

22. **Investment Schedule**

	Date	Amount
(a) Initial Investment		$
(b) Subsequent Investment(s)		$
		$
		$
(c) Expected date that normal operations will begin:		

3) OPIC, as an agency of the U.S. Government, does not support projects that involve illicit payments.

Part 6: U.S. Economic Contribution of the Project

By statute, and consistent with overall U.S. government policy, OPIC does not participate in projects subject to performance requirements that would substantially reduce the potential U.S. trade benefits of the investment. Therefore, for each project, OPIC conducts a review of the potential impact of the investment on the U.S. economy.

When average annual amounts are requested, please provide amounts based on the first five years the project is operational, beginning on the date project construction will be complete and normal operations begin. If your investment is an expansion or privatization of an existing enterprise, please provide only the incremental effects (i.e., the effects–such as procurement or revenues–directly related to the new investment, and not previous or future investments).

23. **Sources of Project Funding (total project cost)**

	Equity	Debt	Other[4]
(a) From the Investor:	$	$	$
(b) From other U.S. Investors:	$	$	$
(c) From Host Country Investors:	$	$	$
(d) From third country investors or international institutions (specify):			
	$	$	$
	$	$	$
	$	$	$
	$	$	$
(e) **Total** (= total project cost)	$	$	$

24. **Offshore Funds**

Of the project funding listed in 23 (a) and (b) above, what amount, if any, is from an offshore source. For example, what amount of U.S. funds will not flow from the U.S. to the host country, but rather from another country (such as from a foreign bank account owned by the U.S. entity)?

$ _____

4) For example, technical assistance or management service agreements, leases, or consigned equipment.

25. Use of Project Funds

Initial Project Expenditures in Column 1 refers to the costs included in Question 23(e) above, including land, buildings, raw materials, equipment, labor, services, working capital and other costs.

Subsequent Procurement in Column 2 refers to the average annual value over the first five years of procurement necessary for the project's continued operation, including raw materials, labor, services, working capital and other costs that are generally funded by the project's revenues.

	Column 1 Initial Project Expenditures	Column 2 Subsequent Procurement
(a) Purchased or spent in the host country[5]	$	$
(b) Purchased from the United States[6]	$	$
(c) Purchased from other developing countries (specify):		
	$	$
	$	$
	$	$
(d) Purchased from other industrialized countries (specify):		
	$	$
	$	$
	$	$
(e) Total[7]	$	$

5) Indicate any host country procurement consisting of fees that are also counted in Question 28 (a) below.

6) OPIC considers U.S. procurement to be equipment manufactured by, or services provided by, U.S. workers. Equipment or services sourced from U.S. subsidiaries overseas should be listed in 25 (c) or (d) above. Indicate what amounts and categories of funds spent in the U.S. for debt financing, lease payments or fees are also accounted for in Question 26 below.

7) Initial Project Expenditures should equal total figure given for 23 (e).

BUSINESS CONFIDENTIAL INFORMATION

26. Initial Procurement from the United States

Please list items procured from the U.S. for initial project expenditures from Question 25(b), column 1, above.

	Type of Good/Service	Manufacturer	City and State	Dollar Amount	New/Used	Minority Owned	Women Owned
(a)				$	☐ New ☐ Used	☐ Yes ☐ No	☐ Yes ☐ No
(b)				$	☐ New ☐ Used	☐ Yes ☐ No	☐ Yes ☐ No
(c)				$	☐ New ☐ Used	☐ Yes ☐ No	☐ Yes ☐ No
(d)				$	☐ New ☐ Used	☐ Yes ☐ No	☐ Yes ☐ No
(e)				$	☐ New ☐ Used	☐ Yes ☐ No	☐ Yes ☐ No
(f)				$	☐ New ☐ Used	☐ Yes ☐ No	☐ Yes ☐ No

27. Subsequent Procurement from the United States

Please list items procured from the U.S. for initial project expenditures from Question 25(b), column 2, above.

	Type of Good/Service	Manufacturer	City and State	Dollar Amount	New/Used	Minority Owned	Women Owned
(a)				$	☐ New ☐ Used	☐ Yes ☐ No	☐ Yes ☐ No
(b)				$	☐ New ☐ Used	☐ Yes ☐ No	☐ Yes ☐ No
(c)				$	☐ New ☐ Used	☐ Yes ☐ No	☐ Yes ☐ No
(d)				$	☐ New ☐ Used	☐ Yes ☐ No	☐ Yes ☐ No
(e)				$	☐ New ☐ Used	☐ Yes ☐ No	☐ Yes ☐ No
(f)				$	☐ New ☐ Used	☐ Yes ☐ No	☐ Yes ☐ No

28. Destination of Project's Sales or Production

Estimate the project's average annual direct sales revenues by country. If project production involves more than one product, please list the products in an attachment and specify a percentage breakdown by product. If project production will be used as a component or other input into another product, indicate the final destination and value of that product.

average annual direct sales

(a) Sold in host country: $

(b) Exported to the United States: $

(c) Exported to other countries (specify):

_____ $

_____ $

_____ $

29. Financial Returns to the United States

Please indicate average annual remittances over the first five years of project operations.

(a) Financial Returns to the United States[8]

    i. Loan principal and interest: $

    ii. Lease payments: $

    iii. Dividends or profits: $

    iv. Returns of capital (partial / total disinvestments): $

    v. Fees (license, royalties, technical assistance, etc.): $

(b) Remittances to third countries (i.e., not to the U.S. or host country): $

Part 7: Developmental Effects

30. Human Capacity Building

Indicate the number of persons employed by the project during project construction (if applicable) and at fifth year of operation. If the project is an expansion, include employment resulting only from this expansion of the enterprise.

	Management		Professional/Technical		Unskilled Labor	
	Construction	5th Year	Construction	5th Year	Construction	5th Year
Local						
Expatriate						
Total						

8) This includes funds returning to the United States only. Do not include funds going to U.S. accounts overseas.

(a) For the non-construction jobs listed above, indicate the percentage that will receive formal training.

Management	%	Professional/Technical	%	Unskilled Labor	%

(b) Will the project provide training outside of the host country?   ☐ Yes   ☐ No

    If <u>Yes</u>, please indicate countries where training will take place:

31. Private Sector Development

(a) What will be the percentage of local ownership of the project at the start of operations?   %

(b) If there is local ownership, is the local owner a small or medium enterprise?
    ☐ Yes   ☐ No

(c) Will the project encourage private ownership, such as through privatization or creation of opportunities for individual property (including home) ownership?
    ☐ Yes   ☐ No

32. Leveraging Impacts

(a) Will the project involve other federal, regional, or multilateral organizations (e.g., AID, TDA, IFC, or MIGA)?

    If Yes, please explain:

(b) Will the project involve a public-private partnership (e.g., through local development bank, ministry or NGO)?
    ☐ Yes   ☐ No

    If Yes, please explain:

33. Social Effects (Good Corporate Citizenship)

(a) Does the project company have an equal employment policy over and above the local law that will be applied to the proposed investment? Such a policy would cover gender, ethnicity, and social affiliation.
    ☐ Yes   ☐ No

    If Yes, please explain:

(b) Will there be any benefits or policies in place that specifically address the needs of women in the workplace?
    ☐ Yes   ☐ No

    If Yes, please explain:

(c) Will the project benefit a poor (e.g., rural) region of the host country?

☐ Yes   ☐ No

If Yes, please explain:

(d) Will the project extend benefits to its employees (e.g., healthcare, daily meals, transportation or housing)?

☐ Yes   ☐ No

If Yes, please explain:

(e) Will the project provide benefits to the local community (e.g., recreational facilities, community center, schools or medical clinics)?

☐ Yes   ☐ No

If Yes, please explain:

(f) Does the project directly restore or preserve the environment (e.g., pollution reduction, ecotourism, reforestation, water treatment, wildlife conservation)?

☐ Yes   ☐ No

If Yes, please explain:

34. Developmental Infrastructure Improvements

(a) Will the project strengthen the **physical infrastructure** of the host country (e.g., communications, power, transportation)?

☐ Yes   ☐ No

If Yes, please explain:

(b) Will the project strengthen the **financial infrastructure** of the host country (e.g., micro-finance, on-lending, mortgage lending, or financial market development)?

☐ Yes   ☐ No

If Yes, please explain:

(c) Will the project strengthen the **social infrastructure** of the host country (e.g., nutrition, shelter, water and sanitation, health, or education)?

☐ Yes   ☐ No

If Yes, please explain:

(d) If you answered Yes to any of the above questions, please indicate the economic status of the user population.

---

35. **Macroeconomic and Institutional Effects**

Estimate average annual revenues (duties, taxes, or other payments) to the host government resulting from the project's first five year's of operation. If any amount listed includes host country procurement that is also counted in Question 25 (a), Column 2, please so indicate.

(a) Duties, taxes, or other payments: $ _____

(b) Duties and taxes lost as a result of the investment: $ _____
    (e.g., due to import substitution)

(c) Is the investment being implemented in the context of a government regulatory, judicial, or other institutional reform program?

☐ Yes   ☐ No

If Yes, please describe the reforms.

(d) As a result or condition of this investment, will the government implement regulatory, judicial or other institutional reforms?

☐ Yes   ☐ No

36. **Technology and Knowledge Transfer/Competitive Impacts**

(a) Will the project introduce innovative management practices?

☐ Yes   ☐ No

If Yes, please explain:

(b) Will the project bring new marketing and distribution strategies to the host country?

☐ Yes   ☐ No

If Yes, please explain:

(c) Will the project apply new production technology for the first time?

☐ Yes   ☐ No

If Yes, please explain:

(d) Will the project market products available for the first time?

☐ Yes   ☐ No

If Yes, please explain:

(e) Will the project lower local prices?

☐ Yes   ☐ No

If Yes, please explain:

(f) Will the project contribute to the economic diversification of the host country?

☐ Yes   ☐ No

If Yes, please explain:

Part 8: Worker Rights

OPIC is required by statute to ensure that the project will not contribute to violations of internationally recognized worker rights. These rights are defined to include:

(a) freedom of association;

(b) the right to organize and bargain collectively;

(c) prohibition of forced or compulsory labor;

(d) minimum age for employment; and

(e) acceptable conditions of work with respect to minimum wages, hours of work and occupational health and safety.

All OPIC political risk insurance contracts include language to ensure that the project is operated in accordance with internationally recognized worker rights. Since host country labor laws and practices vary, this language may be supplemented on a case-by-case basis to ensure that the project does not contribute to worker rights violations in the host country.

37. **Will the Investor have sufficient control over labor-management relations to ensure that the project does not contribute to violations of worker rights as defined above?**

    ☐ Yes   ☐ No

    If <u>No</u>, please explain:

38. **If investing in, lending to, or acquiring an existing enterprise, is the work force organized in a trade union?**

    ☐ Yes   ☐ No

    (a) If you answered <u>Yes</u>, is the trade union recognized by the management?   ☐ Yes   ☐ No

    (b) If you answered <u>Yes</u>, is the trade union recognized by the host government?   ☐ Yes   ☐ No

39. **If investing in a new enterprise or existing enterprise with a non-unionized work force, does the Investor anticipate that the work force will be unionized?**

    ☐ Yes   ☐ No

    Please Explain:

Part 9: Insurance of Exports Certification

40. **OPIC seeks to ensure that American insurance companies have an opportunity to compete for transportation insurance business associated with the export of goods to projects supported by OPIC programs. To encourage fair and open competition for this business, OPIC requires certain certifications from Investors receiving OPIC insurance. Please check the appropriate box below:**

    (a) No certification is required if an Investor receiving OPIC insurance **does not have** a controlling interest in the project in which it is investing.[9] If your firm does not have a controlling interest in the project, please check the box below and proceed to the next Section.

    ☐ The Investor **does not have** a controlling interest in the project.

    (see next page for options b and c).

---

9) A "controlling interest" means that the Investor has a majority equity interest in the project or can exercise effective management control by agreement or otherwise.

164 TRADE FINANCE HANDBOOK

BUSINESS CONFIDENTIAL INFORMATION

(b) In those instances where the Investor **does have** a controlling interest in the project, OPIC requires that the Investor certify that each contract for the export of goods from the United States in connection with the establishment of the project will include a clause requiring that United States insurance companies shall have a fair and open competitive opportunity to provide insurance against risk of loss for such export of goods. If Investor is able to so certify, please check the box below.

☐ I certify that each contract for the export of goods from the United States in connection with the establishment of the project will include a clause requiring that U.S. insurance companies shall have a fair and open competitive opportunity to provide insurance against risk of loss for such exports.

(c) In those instances where the Investor **does have** a controlling interest in the project, but is unable to provide the certification requested in Question 40 (b) above, please check the appropriate box below.

☐ The project country prohibits use of U.S. insurance services for transportation insurance.

☐ There are no exports associated with the establishment of this project.

☐ All transportation insurance associated with the export of U.S. goods to the project is or will be arranged through the Investor's pre-existing worldwide insurance program, for which U.S. insurance companies were given a fair and open opportunity to compete. It is not practicable to alter these arrangements for U.S. exports to the project.

☐ Other (*please explain*):

Part 10: Foreign Narcotics Kingpin Act Certification

By law (the Foreign Narcotics Kingpin Act, 24 U.S.C. 1901-1908 (the "Act") and Executive Order 12978 (the "Executive Order"), OPIC is prohibited from engaging in a transaction involving (i) persons designated by the President of the United States as significant foreign narcotics traffickers ("SDNTKs") or anyone who in any way aids or abets a SDNTK and (ii) any person designated by the Office of Foreign Assets Control ("OFAC") of the U.S. Department of Treasury as a specially designated narcotics trafficker ("SDNTs") or anyone who in any way aids or abets a SDNT and is required to use diligence to ensure that it is not, in supporting a project, doing so. To comply with its statutory obligations under the Act and the Executive Order, OPIC requires certification, by signing this form, that to the best of your knowledge and belief, after due inquiry, none of the participants, or proposed participants in the transaction is a SDNTK or an SDNT or an aider or abettor thereof.[10]

Applicant certifies that, to the best of its knowledge and belief, after due inquiry, no participant or likely participant, in the transaction for which the undersigned has requested OPIC political risk insurance is designated by OFAC as an SDNTK or an SDNT, or an aider or abettor thereof. Applicant further certifies that, to the best of its knowledge and belief, after due inquiry, Applicant is in compliance with all requirements of the Act and the Executive Order.

10) Participant includes, but is not limited to, corporations and their shareholders, officers, and directors; partnerships and their partners; limited liability companies and their members; limited liability partnerships and their partners; trustees and beneficiaries of trusts, lenders, joint venturers in any way participating in the transaction for which political risk insurance is requested, including, but not limited to, sponsors, investors, the foreign enterprise, and O&M and EPC contractors of the foreign enterprise. The names of persons designated as SDNTKs and SDNTs may be determined by contacting OFAC at (202) 622-2490 or by viewing a listing of SDNTKs and SDNTs on the OFAC web site (www.ustreas.gov/ofac/). The names of persons designated as SDNTKs and SDNTs may be determined by contacting OFAC at (202) 622-2490 or by viewing a listing of SDNTKs and SDNTs on the OFAC web site (www.ustreas.gov/ofac/).

OPIC - 52

14

Part 11: Additional Information

Depending on the type of project for which OPIC insurance is being requested and the country in which it is located, OPIC may request additional information, including, but not limited to, the following:

Environmental Effects

Most OPIC political risk insurance contracts include language to ensure that the project is operated in accordance with World Bank and local standards. For projects that have the potential to result in adverse and/or significant environmental impacts, OPIC will require the Investor to 1) provide information sufficient for OPIC to complete an adequate environmental review or 2) submit an environmental impact assessment, and the environmental requirements in the OPIC contract may be supplemented as appropriate.

Worker Safety

OPIC must ensure that projects receiving its support do not have a major or unreasonable adverse effect on worker safety and may request information regarding training, equipment, and applicable health and safety standards at the project.

Economic Effects

Depending on the type of project for which OPIC support is requested, OPIC may require further information regarding the effect of the project on the host country's development and on the U.S. economy.

Developmental Effects

OPIC may request additional information on the positive impact of the project on the host country development, including any infrastructure development, the quality and availability of comparable products, procurement from local businesses, employee training, etc.

Part 12: Signature

Each Investor must sign this application.

Applicant (*Investor*): _____   Applicant (*Investor*): _____

By: _____   By: _____

Name & Title (*print*): _____   Name & Title (*print*): _____

Date: _____   Date: _____

By signing this form, the Investor(s) hereby represents and warrants that (a) this form is identical in all material and substantive respects to OMB form No. 3420 0011 sent to the Investor by OPIC and (b) that the Investor understands that OPIC shall regard the Investor's answers to the questions on this form to be answers to the questions as asked on OMB form No. 3420 0011.

Dear Investor:

Attached is the Application Form for financing from the Overseas Private Investment Corporation (OPIC). OPIC's mission is to act as a financial catalyst for viable developmental projects in over 150 countries and areas around the world.

The Application Form is just one component of an Application Package that must be completed in order to be considered. A full Application Package is made up of:
1. The Application Form,
2. A business plan (See Attachment I "Key Elements in a Business Plan),
3. Financial statements of the sponsor and project (if operating),
4. A diagram of the project's ownership structure,
5. Financial projections of the project's future operations,
6. Any commercial or financial agreements related to the project (if applicable), and
7. A Sponsor Disclosure Report (OPIC Form 129) for each entity considered to be a sponsor.

   (Other supporting material may include feasibility studies, marketing studies and environmental studies.)

The information requested in the Application Form will allow OPIC to determine whether the proposed project and its sponsors meet the basic *eligibility criteria* and *policy requirements* for OPIC financing. For consideration, a complete Application Package must be submitted. Questions on the application can be directed to OPIC's Investment Development Department at 202-336-8627 or apply@opic.gov.

We look forward to working with you on your financing needs.

OPIC 115
OMB No. 3420-0015
Exp. 12/31/07

APPLICATION FOR FINANCING

OVERSEAS PRIVATE INVESTMENT CORPORATION (OPIC)
(An Agency of the United States Government)
1100 New York Avenue, NW
Washington, D.C. 20527
Phone: (202) 336-8400
Fax: (202) 408-9866

GENERAL INFORMATION

This application is to be used to apply for OPIC financing[1], as authorized by the Foreign Assistance Act of 1961, as amended.

All information furnished in this application is treated as **privileged business information**, to the fullest extent permitted by law or subject to other authority. The application consists of the following parts:

Part A:	Summary Information
Part B:	Sponsor and Project Information
Part C:	U.S. Effects of the Project
Part D:	Host Country Developmental Effects of the Project
Part E:	Environment/Worker Safety/Worker Rights
Part F:	Signatures
Part G:	Information Checklist

Sponsors should have developed all or most of the information requested herein prior to submitting a formal application for financing. Responses to questions, which call for estimates or projections, should take the form of good faith statements made to the best of the applicant's knowledge and belief. This application form must be signed and dated by the principal U.S. sponsors.

In addition to the Application Form 115, a complete application package must be submitted in order for OPIC to consider this loan request. A full application package (see Part G) is made up of a business plan (see Attachment I: Key Elements in a Business Plan), financial statements of the sponsor and project (if operating), financial projections of future operations, any offtake agreements (if applicable) and a Sponsor Disclosure Report for each entity considered to be a sponsor (Sponsor Disclosure Report available at www.opic.gov/forms/forms.htm).

Please note that after the initial review of this application further information may be required.

---

[1] For helpful guidance in how to fill out this application, please see **Guidelines for the Application for Financing** (OPIC 115 Supplement). This supplement also provides information on the mechanics of the application process, business plan components, timing and fees, as well as a glossary of pertinent finance terms.

2

Submission
Any supporting documents that can be attached in an email format should be sent to
apply@opic.gov.

Any supporting documentation that is not available in electronic formal should be mailed to

Investment Development and Economic Growth Department
Overseas Private Investment Corporation
1100 New York Avenue, N.W.
Washington, D.C. 20527
Phone: (202) 336-8627
Fax: (202) 408-5155
Email: apply@opic.gov

Please Note: NEITHER SUBMISSION NOR ACCEPTANCE OF THIS APPLICATION IMPLIES THAT
THE PROJECT IS ELIGIBLE FOR FINANCING OR THAT FINANCING WILL BE PROVIDED.

APPLICATION FOR FINANCING

OVERSEAS PRIVATE INVESTMENT CORPORATION (OPIC)
(An agency of the United States Government)
1100 New York Avenue, NW
Washington, D.C. 20527

PART A: SUMMARY INFORMATION	
1	Project country:
2	Name of Project Company (i.e., foreign enterprise):
3	Industry/type of project:
4	U.S. sponsor(s):
5	Total project costs: $
6	Proposed OPIC loan amount: $
7	Name of OPIC staff with whom you have discussed this project:

PART B: SPONSOR AND PROJECT INFORMATION

Please answer Question B1 and B2 for each sponsor of the project.

1	SPONSOR AND CONTACTS
a	Sponsor or company name:
	Address:
	City: State: Zip or Postal Code:
	Country:
	Telephone: Fax: e-mail:
b	Type of business or industry:	c	Percentage of Sponsor's ownership in project company: %
d	Name of person OPIC should contact for information:
	Title:
	Telephone: Fax: e-mail:
e	Name of authorized representative (e.g. corporate representative, attorney, financial advisor, etc.) if applicable:
	Title:
	Address:
	City: State: Zip or Postal Code: Country:
	Telephone: Fax: e-mail:

2	SPONSOR STATUS (Please indicate the legal form of the sponsor(s) indicated in Question B1 in the appropriate section below.)		
a	☐ U.S. Corporation ☐ Public ☐ Private ☐ Sub-Chapter S Corporation		
	I	Date and place of incorporation:	
	II	Is more than 50% of each class of shares of the corporation beneficially owned by U.S. citizens?	☐ Yes ☐ No
b	☐ U.S. Partnership or Association		
	I	Organized under the laws of (state or territory):	
	II	Is more than 50% of the partnership or association beneficially owned by U.S. citizens?	☐ Yes ☐ No

c	☐ Individual	Citizenship:
d	☐ Foreign Corporation, partnership or other association	
	I	Name of single largest holder:
	II	Largest holder's place of organization (country of citizenship if an individual):
	III	Percentage of ownership by largest single holder:
e	Is the Sponsor a women-owned or minority-owned company? ☐ Yes ☐ No	

3 PROJECT COMPANY

a	Project company name:
	Address:
	City: Country:
	Telephone: Fax: e-mail:
b	Legal form of organization (corporation, branch, partnership, etc.):
c	Place and date of organization:
d	Please provide a **_detailed_** description of the project. Include a specific description of any and all products or services that the project will produce or provide (i.e. *"fiber optic cable"*, not *"telecommunication equipment"*).
e	Is this a new project or an expansion of an existing project? ☐ New ☐ Expansion
f	Location of project if different than address:

PRIVILEGED BUSINESS INFORMATION

The following Parts C, D, and E of the application request information, which is required by OPIC's governing legislation. The information provided will allow OPIC to determine whether a project and its sponsor(s) meet the eligibility criteria for OPIC financing with regard to the effects of the project on the U.S. economy and on the environment and development abroad. Complete responses are mandatory, per the Foreign Assistance Act of 1961, as amended, Section 231(k)(2).

PART C: EFFECTS OF THE PROJECT ON THE U.S. ECONOMY

1 PROJECT AFFILIATION

Does the project sponsor have any affiliates? If yes, please list them in the space provided below	❏ Yes ❏ No

2 PROJECT CATEGORY

If your project falls into one of the categories listed below, please check the appropriate box and Skip to Question 7 (Sources of Project Financing). If not, check the "Not Applicable" box to the right and proceed to Question 3.	❏ Not Applicable

❏ Financial services (e.g., a branch bank, leasing company, etc.) intended to serve predominantly host country or regional markets

❏ Telecommunications services intended to serve predominantly host country or regional markets.

❏ Oil and/or gas exploration

❏ Tourism services (e.g., a hotel, restaurant or resort).

❏ Power supply or transmission for host country or regional markets

❏ Mining of minerals or ores not mined in the U.S.

❏ Host country or regional sales, service, distribution or transportation (no production involved).

3 PRODUCTION OF COMPARABLE PRODUCTS

a	Does the project sponsor or any affiliate of the project sponsor produce goods or services in the U.S., which are comparable to goods or services produced or to be produced by the project company?	❏ Yes ❏ No
b	If you answered "No" to Question 3 (a), please skip to Question 4. If you answered "Yes" to Question 3 (a), will the project's production compete with or replace such comparable U.S. production?	❏ Yes ❏ No
c	If you answered "No" to Question 3 (b), please explain below why the project company's production will not compete with or replace such U.S.-based production.	

4 EMPLOYMENT IN COMPARABLE PRODUCTION

For each project sponsor and each affiliate of the sponsor that is producing goods in the U.S. which are comparable to the goods or services which are or will be produced by the project, please indicate the number of U.S. employees engaged in the production of such goods or services: currently, one year ago, and projected one year from now.

Name of Project Sponsor or Affiliate	Current U.S. Employment	U.S. Employment One Year Ago	Projected U.S. Employment One Year

5 EFFECTS ON U.S. OPERATIONS

Has the project sponsor and each affiliate of the project sponsor reduced or does it expect to reduce the number of its U.S. employees or the level of operations in the U.S. either 1) in order to devote resources to the project, or 2) because the project's production enables them to do so? If "Yes", please explain below.	❏ Yes ❏ No

6 EXPORT PROCESSING ZONES

Will the project company be located in export processing zone or designated area in the project country in which the tax, tariff, labor, environment, and safety laws of the project country do not apply, in part or in whole, to the activities carried out within such zone or area?	❏ Yes ❏ No

7 SOURCES OF PROJECT FUNDING (TOTAL PROJECT COST)

		Equity	Debt	Other*
a	From the Investor	$	$	$
b	From other U.S. Investors	$	$	$
c	From host country investors	$	$	$
d	From third country investors or international institutions (specify):	$	$	$
e	FUNDING TOTAL: $	$	$	$

*e.g. technical assistance or management service agreements, leases, consigned equipment, etc.

8 OFFSHORE FUNDS

Of the project funding listed in 7a and b above, what amount, if any, is from an offshore source (i.e., what amount of U.S. funds will not flow from the U.S. to the host country, but rather from another country, for example, a foreign bank account owned by the U.S. entity)?	$

9 USES OF PROJECT FUNDS

Initial Project Expenditures refers to the costs included in Question 7e above, including land, buildings, raw materials, equipment, labor, services, working capital and other costs. *Subsequent Operational Procurement* refers to the average annual value over the first five years of procurement necessary for the project's continued operation, including raw materials, labor, services, working capital and other costs that are generally funded by the project's revenues.

		Initial Project Expenditures (Column 1)	Annual Subsequent Operational Procurement (Column 2)
a	Purchased or spent in the host country	$	$
b	Purchased from the United States*	$	$
c	Purchased from other developing countries (specify):	$	$
d	Purchased from other industrialized countries (specify):	$	$
e	TOTAL: $	$	$

(Note: Column 1 total should equal total figure given for 7e above)
*OPIC considers U.S. procurement to be equipment manufactured by, or services provided by, U.S. workers. Equipment or services sourced from U.S. subsidiaries overseas should be listed in 9c or d above.

10 U.S. SUPPLIERS INFORMATION

Please provide a detailed list of U.S. manufacturers supplying key goods and services for the project

a	**Initial Procurement:** *Please list items to be procured from the United States for initial project expenditures from Question 9b, Column 1, above. **Also ensure that the total in 9b, Column 1, equals the total in 10a, below.***

Manufacturer	City and State	Product		Procurement Amount ($)
			❑New ❑Used	
			❑New ❑Used	
			❑New ❑Used	
			❑New ❑Used	
			❑New ❑Used	
			❑New ❑Used	
			❑New ❑Used	
			TOTAL	

b	**On-going Capital Expenditures (Purchase Price Average Annual Over 5 Years):** *Please list items to be procured from the United States for subsequent annual project operations from Question 9b, Column 2, above. **Also ensure that the total in 9b, Column 2, equals the total in 10b, below.***

Manufacturer	City and State	Product		Procurement Amount ($)
			❑New ❑Used	
			❑New ❑Used	
			❑New ❑Used	
			❑New ❑Used	
			❑New ❑Used	
			❑New ❑Used	
			❑New ❑Used	
			TOTAL	

11 DESTINATION OF PROJECT SALES AND PRODUCTION

In column 1, estimate the project's average annual direct sales revenue by country over the first five years of operations. **If project production involves more than one product, please list all products on an attachment and specify a percentage breakdown by product.** In column 2, if project production will be used as a component or other input into another product, indicate the final destination and value of sales of that product. **If the investment is an expansion of an existing enterprise, or otherwise only part of an enterprise, only the incremental revenues related to and resulting from the new investment should be provided.**

	AVERAGE ANNUAL REVENUES FOR FIRST 5 YEARS OF PROJECT OPERATIONS	
	Column 1 Initial Destination Total Revenues ($)	Column 2 Final Destination Sales Value of Final Product ($)
Sold in Host Country		
Exported to the United States		
Exported to other countries:		
Country:		
Country:		
Country:		
Country:		
Country:		
TOTALS		

12 IMPORT SUBSTITUTION

Will the project company's production that is sold in the host country replace current imports?	☐Yes ☐No	
If yes, what is the average annual value of the imports replaced?	$	

13 EXPORTS TO THE UNITED STATES

Will project exports to the United States replace products currently exported from the host or other countries to the U.S. market?	☐Yes ☐No	
If yes, what is the average annual value of the exports replaced?	$	

14 AVERAGE ANNUAL FINANCIAL OUTFLOW FROM THE HOST COUNTRY OVER THE FIRST 5 YEARS OF OPERATION

	In each column, estimate the project's average annual financial outflow from the host country to the respective destinations.	Remittance to the United States	Remittance to Other Countries
a	Total Loan(s) Principal and Interest:	$	$
b	Lease Payment:	$	$
c	Dividends or Profits:	$	$
d	Return on Capital:	$	$
e	Fees:	$	$
f	Other:	$	$

15 U.S. EXPORT SUBSTITUTIONS

a		Will any of the project company's production sold within the host country or to third-country markets replace U.S. exports?	☐Yes ☐No	
b	I	If yes, estimate the average annual amount of displaced exports previously exported to the host country:	$	
	II	If yes, estimate the average annual amount of displaced exports previously exported to third countries:	$	
c		In the absence of this investment, would other factors have caused this displacement of U.S. exports?	☐Yes ☐No	
		If yes, please explain.		

16 PERFORMANCE REQUIREMENTS

Describe any host government decrees, laws, directives or agreements with the Investor or Foreign Enterprise that might affect project imports, exports, or employment *(e.g., local content or export requirements, trade balancing or local hiring requirements, etc.)*.

PRIVILEGED BUSINESS INFORMATION

PART D: HOST COUNTRY DEVELOPMENTAL EFFECTS

1 HUMAN CAPACITY BUILDING

a	Indicate the estimated number of persons to be employed by the project during construction (if applicable) and by the fifth year of operation. If the project is an expansion, include only employment resulting from the expansion.						
	Management		Professional/Technical		Unskilled Labor		
	Construction	5th Year	Construction	5th Year	Construction	5th Year	
Local:							
Expatriate:							
Total:							

b	For the non-construction jobs identified above, indicate the percentage that will receive <u>formal</u> training in each category:			
	Management	%	Professional/Technical	%	Unskilled Labor	%
c	Will the project provide training outside of the host country? If yes, please indicate countries:	☐Yes ☐No

2 PRIVATE SECTOR DEVELOPMENT

a	What will be the percentage of local ownership of the project at the start of operations?	%
b	If there is local ownership, is the local owner a Small & Medium Enterprise (SME)?[2]	☐Yes ☐No
c	Will the project encourage private ownership, such as through privatization, or creation of opportunities for individual property (including home) ownership? If yes, please explain.	☐Yes ☐No

3 LEVERAGING IMPACTS

a	Will the project involve other federal/regional/multilateral organizations (such as AID, TDA, IFC, MIGA, etc.)? If Yes, please list organizations:	☐Yes ☐No
b	Will the project involve a public-private partnership (e.g. thru local development bank/ministry/NGO)? If yes, please explain.	☐Yes ☐No

4 SOCIAL EFFECTS (GOOD CORPORATE CITIZENSHIP)

a	Does the project company have an equal employment policy over and above the local law that will be applied to the proposed investment? Such a policy would cover gender, ethnicity, and social affiliation. If yes, please explain.	☐Yes ☐No
b	Will there be any benefits or policies in place that specifically address the needs of women at the workplace? (Examples are childcare, maternity leave, non-harassment policies)? If Yes, please explain.	☐Yes ☐No
c	Will the project benefit a poor (e.g., rural) region of the host country? If Yes, please explain.	☐Yes ☐No
d	Will the project extend company benefits to its employees? If Yes, please explain. (e.g., *health coverage, daily meals, transportation, or housing assistance*)	☐Yes ☐No
e	Will the project provide benefits to the local community? If Yes, please explain. (e.g., *recreational facilities, community center, schools, or medical clinics*)	☐Yes ☐No
f	Does the project directly restore or preserve the environment? If Yes, please explain. (e.g., *pollution reduction, eco-tourism, reforestation, water treatment (clean-up), or wildlife conservation*)	☐Yes ☐No

5 DEVELOPMENTAL INFRASTRUCTURE IMPROVEMENTS

a	Will the project strengthen the *physical* infrastructure of the host country? (e.g., communications, power, transportation)	☐Yes ☐No
b	Will the project strengthen the *financial* infrastructure of the host country? If Yes, please explain. (e.g., microfinance, on-lending, mortgage lending, or financial market development)	☐Yes ☐No
c	Will the project strengthen the *social* infrastructure of the host country? (e.g., nutrition, shelter, water & sanitation, health, or education)	☐Yes ☐No
	If you answered Yes to any of the above questions, please indicate the economic status of the user population.	

---

[2] <u>Small- and Medium Enterprise (SME)</u>: Up to 300 employees, total assets of up to $15 million, and total annual sales of up to $15 million. (*IFC*)

6 MACROECONOMIC & INSTITUTIONAL EFFECTS

a	Estimate the average annual revenues (duties, taxes or other payments) of the host government resulting from the project's first five years of operations.	
b	Duties, taxes, and other payments:	$
c	Duties and taxes lost as a result of the investment (e.g. because of import substitution):	$
d	Duration of tax holiday, if any:	
e	Is the investment being implemented *in the context of* a government regulatory, judicial or other institutional reform program? If Yes, please describe the reform program.	☐Yes ☐No
f	*As a result or condition of this investment*, will the government implement regulatory, judicial or other institutional reforms? If Yes, please describe the reforms.	☐Yes ☐No

7 TECHNOLOGY & KNOWLEDGE TRANSFER/PRODUCTIVITY ENHANCEMENT INTIATIVES

a	Will the project introduce innovative management practices? If Yes, please explain.	☐Yes ☐No
b	Will the project bring new marketing and distribution strategies to the host country? If Yes, please explain.	☐Yes ☐No
c	Will the project apply new production technology for the first time? If Yes, please explain.	☐Yes ☐No
d	Will the project market products available for the first time? If Yes, please explain.	☐Yes ☐No
e	Will the project lower local prices? If Yes, please explain.	☐Yes ☐No
f	Will the project contribute to the economic diversification of the host country? If Yes, please explain.	☐Yes ☐No

PART E: ENVIRONMENTAL EFFECTS, WORKER SAFETY, AND WORKER RIGHTS

1 INDUSTRIAL, CHEMICAL AND MECHANICAL PROCESSES

List all significant industrial, chemical, and mechanical processes associated with the project.

2 POTENTIAL ADVERSE ENVIRONMENTAL EFFECTS

What potentially adverse effects could the project have on the environment, worker health and safety, or endangered species?

3 CONTROL OVER PROJECT DESIGN AND OPERATION

Will the project sponsor have significant control over the design and operation of the project to mitigate any such adverse effects? If Yes, please explain.	☐Yes ☐No

4 MEASURES TO PREVENT ADVERSE EFFECTS

What measures will the project sponsor and the project company take to prevent adverse effects?

5 ENVIRONMENTAL STUDIES OR ASSESSMENTS

List below and attach any environmental studies or assessments that have been done on the project to date.

PRIVILEGED BUSINESS INFORMATION

6	WORKER SAFETY AND WORKER RIGHTS	
a	If there is an existing project company, does it permit its workers to form or join a labor union?	☐Yes ☐No
b	If the project company is an existing project company, are the workers unionized?	☐Yes ☐No
c	Is a collective bargaining agreement in effect?	☐Yes ☐No
d	What is the legal minimum age for employment in the project country?	Age:
e	What is the legal minimum age for employment in hazardous activities?	Age:
f	What are the legal maximum hours of work without payment of overtime?	Hours:
	With overtime?	Hours:
g	Will employees at the project be employed by contractors or subcontractors or will they be employed by the project company?	

PART F: SIGNATURES

Each U.S. sponsor listed in response to Part B Questions #1 and #2 must sign and date this application prior to its submission.

APPLICANT

"Under penalty of law, I certify that the statements and information provided herein are true to and correct to the best of my knowledge and belief."

Sponsor:	By (Signature):	
Print name and title:		Date:

APPLICANT

"Under penalty of law, I certify that the statements and information provided herein are true to and correct to the best of my knowledge and belief."

Sponsor:	By (Signature):	
Print name and title:		Date:

APPLICANT

"Under penalty of law, I certify that the statements and information provided herein are true to and correct to the best of my knowledge and belief."

Sponsor:	By (Signature):	
Print name and title:		Date:

PRIVILEGED BUSINESS INFORMATION

PART G: INFORMATION CHECKLIST		
Items #1-#5 are required by OPIC in order to process this application. Please be sure that all of these items have been assembled and attached or enclosed before signing and submitting this application		
1		Business Plan (Please see Attachment I)
2		Financial Statements and References for Sponsors and Operators

		The financial statements should include a balance sheet, income statement, and cash flow statement (preferably in accordance with U.S. GAAP). Please note below the specific statements and references required for your form of organization.
		
		For a Public Corporation: 1) Audited Financial Statements (most recent 3 years)
		                                       2) 10K and 10Q (most recent)
		
		For a Private Corporation: 1) Financial Statements, Audited (if available) or Unaudited (most recent 3 years)
		                                       2) 3 Bank References
		                                       3) 3 Trade References
		
		For a Partnership: 1) Financial Statements, Audited or Unaudited (most recent 3 years)
		                                       2) General Partner information, including:
		                                          a) Statement of Net Worth (assets and liabilities)
		                                          b) Ownership
		                                          c) 3 Bank References
		                                          d) 3 Trade References
		
		For an Individual: 1) Signed Statement of Net Worth (assets and liabilities)
		                                       2) Bank Statements (most recent 3 months)
		                                       3) Tax Returns (most recent 3 years)
		                                     4) 3 Bank References
		                                       5) 3 Trade References

3		A completed and signed OPIC Sponsor Disclosure Report for each Sponsor (Please see Attachment II)
4		Pro-forma Financial Statements relating to the project
5		A list of all commercial and financial agreements entered into to date relating to the project
SUPPORTING DOCUMENTATION		
6		Feasibility/Marketing Studies
7		Environmental Study(ies)
ADDITIONAL SUPPORTING DOCUMENTATION		
8		Please provide any additional documentation that may be helpful in expediting your application.

KEY ELEMENTS IN A BUSINESS PLAN

Please attach the following supplementary information to the application:

1.   SPONSOR TRACK RECORD
   A.   Please submit at least three years of financial statements (preferably audited). If these are not available, consult OPIC before completing and submitting this application.
   B.   Describe any ownership or participation the sponsor(s) have in other companies located in the host country.

2.   PROJECT OPERATIONAL AND FINANCIAL PLANS
   A.   Describe the current status of the project (including start-up and estimated completion dates, estimated operational start-up date, the status of financing, land and equipment purchases, etc.).
   B.   Please attach a chronology of events regarding the development of the project to date, including joint venture agreement signings (e.g., charter documents, shareholder agreements, etc.), equipment purchases, any studies commissioned or completed, any construction initiated, etc.
   C.   If a marketing study has not been conducted and attached, please describe the market conditions and strategy for the project.
   D.   Please attach supporting financial projections for the project for the life of the proposed OPIC loan, including an income statement, balance sheet, and cash flow statement. Please include detailed assumptions for the projections, including revenue and expense assumptions. This data should be provided on spreadsheets in Excel or other compatible spreadsheet software on a 3.5" computer floppy disk(s). Note: Price, volume, and revenue assumptions should be fully supported and documented including the approximate date and amount of the initial investment, dates and amounts of subsequent investments, and all sources of hard currency revenues that will be used to service the U.S. dollar loan requested from OPIC.
   E.   Indicate who will be managing the day-to day operations of the project.

3.   SOURCES AND USES OF FUNDS
   A.   Please provide a detailed listing outlining of all project cost. These costs may include but are not limited to pre-operating expenses, land, building and improvements, equipment, working capital, and contingencies.
   B.   Indicate sources of funds to finance the project (including both debt and equity). This should include:
      1.   The loan amount and tenor being requested from OPIC.
      2.   Loan amount being requested from other lenders.
      3.   Sources of all project capitalization.
      4.   Capital structure after financing is completed.
   C.   For each loan that is being requested from a lender other than OPIC, indicate loan amount, proposed tenor (including any grace period), and proposed collateral. Describe all loans that are being requested from other lenders including loan amounts, tenor, and proposed collateral.
   D.   If the project is an expansion of an existing enterprise, please also show its capital structure prior to the proposed expansion.
   E.   Provide a detailed description of all source, forms, and dollar values of all equity contributions.
   F.   OPIC typically requires mortgages, liens, pledge of shares, and project completion guaranties to secure its loans. If these are not adequate, additional collateral or guaranties may be required. Please describe the loan collateral (including guaranties), that is proposed to secure an OPIC loan. If required by OPIC could the project sponsor provide a letter of credit to support the project completion guaranty(ies)?

4.   AGREEMENTS, CONTRACTS AND LITIGATION
   A.   Describe any host government incentives and protection (e.g. import tariffs, duties, quotas, prohibitions, subsidies, tax holidays, etc.) applicable generally or specifically to the project company.
   B.   List all licenses, contracts, or other agreements (e.g., pricing, raw materials supplies, bank account approvals, etc.) between the host country government and those sponsor or project company. Attach copies of all listed agreements to this application. Please note the status of those agreements that remain to be finalized or approved.
   C.   Describe any host government decrees, laws, directives, or agreements with the sponsor(s) or project company that might affect project imports or exports, or its ability to operate as a going concern. For example, is the project required to source raw materials locally, to export a minimum percentage of production, or to export sufficient production to offset the foreign exchange costs of imported components? Are there specific tax laws that apply to the project? Are there special agreements that, for example, relate to the sale of natural resources? What laws/decrees specific to the industry may affect the structure of the project?
   D.   Describe all current or pending disputes or litigation involving this project or the project company.
   E.   List any and all agreements to be entered into pertaining to the operation of the project and responsibilities of the sponsors.

APPLICATION FOR IRREVOCABLE COMMERCIAL LETTER OF CREDIT

Bank Use Only

To: **NationalCity®**   **Please check applicable Bank.**

L/C #:_____   Date ___ / ___ / ___

☐ National City Bank
International Operations
P.O. Box 5101
Cleveland, OH 44101-0101
Telephone: (216) 488-7530
(800) 622-8074

☐ National City Bank
International Operations
155 East Broad St.
Columbus, OH 43251-0046

☐ National City Bank
of Michigan/Illinois
International Operations
1001 South Worth
3rd Floor
Birmingham, MI 48009

☐ National City Bank
of Indiana
International Operations
One National City Center
Suite 200E
Indianapolis, IN 46255

☐ National City Bank
of Pennsylvania
International Operations
20 Stanwix Street
Pittsburgh, PA 15222

☐ National City Bank
of Kentucky
International Operations
101 South Fifth Street
Louisville, KY 40202

Please issue an irrevocable commercial letter of credit substantially in accordance with this Application and transmit it as indicated below. In issuing the Credit you are expressly authorized to make such changes from the terms hereinbelow set forth as you, in your sole discretion, may deem advisable provided that no such changes shall vary the principal terms hereof.

For delivery to the beneficiary by: ☐ Courier   ☐ Airmail   ☐ Transmission

Advising Bank:

For Account of (Applicant):

In Favor of (Beneficiary):

Amount:

Drafts to be presented on or before _____ (Expiry date)

(In Country of Beneficiary unless otherwise indicated)

Available by drafts at _____ drawn on you or your correspondent for _____ % of invoice value when accompanied by the following documents:

☐ Beneficiary's signed Commercial Invoice in original and _____ copies
☐ One original packing list and _____ copy(ies)
☐ Special Customs Invoice
☐ Certificate of Origin (Form A if applicable)
☐ Insurance Policy or certificates covering all risks, including war risks, for at least 110% of full invoice value
Transport Document(s): (If more than one is shown, any will be freely accepted, unless otherwise indicated.)
☐ Forwarders/Cargo Receipt in duplicate plus _____ copies
☐ Full set clean on board ocean Bills of Lading plus _____ non-negotiable copies
☐ Original Air Waybill plus _____ copies
☐ Other (Specify): _____

Consignee:
☐ To order Shipper blank endorsed
☐ Consigned to: _____
☐ To order of: _____
Notify:

Marked freight ☐ Prepaid ☐ Collect

Transport documents to be issued by (if specific carrier/forwarder desired): _____

☐ Other Documents:

Covering merchandise described in the invoice as: (Brief description without excessive detail)

Shipping Terms: ☐ CIF ☐ CFR ☐ CIP ☐ FOB ☐ FCA ☐ Other: _____
Name of city/port: _____
From: _____
To: _____
Latest Shipping Date: _____

INSURED BY: ☐ Buyer ☐ Seller

Partial Shipments ☐ permitted, ☐ prohibited

Transshipments ☐ permitted, ☐ prohibited

Special conditions
☐ This letter of credit is transferable.
☐ Banking charges other than issuing bank's for account of ☐ applicant, ☐ beneficiary, ☐ other: _____
☐ Discount charges for account of the ☐ applicant, ☐ beneficiary
☐ Acceptance charges for account of ☐ applicant, ☐ beneficiary
☐ Documents must be presented to Paying/Negotiating bank within _____ days after date of shipment and within validity of letter of credit.
☐ Invoice must state merchandise is in accordance with:
A) Pro Forma Invoice # _____ Dated __ / __ / ____
B) Purchase Order # _____ Dated __ / __ / ____

CREDIT WILL BE SUBJECT TO THE UNIFORM CUSTOMS AND PRACTICE FOR DOCUMENTARY CREDITS OF THE INTERNATIONAL CHAMBER OF COMMERCE IN EFFECT ON THE DATE OF ISSUANCE.

71-0073-00 (Rev. 08/02)

INSURANCE COVERED BY OURSELVES UNLESS INSURANCE DOCUMENT IS SPECIFIED HERIN. WE AGREE TO KEEP INSURANCE COVERAGE IN FORCE UNTIL THIS TRANSACTION IS COMPLETED.

Documents to be delivered in one transmittal, unless otherwise indicated under Special Conditions.

Other Documents required: (continued)

Special Conditions:

Additional instructions to issuing bank, not to be included in the Letter of Credit:

Shipping documents are to be sent by you upon payment/acceptance to: _____

                                                                     (Name)

_____
                                              (Address)

To Pay fees/drawings under the Credit we authorize you or your correspondent bank to debit our account number as stipulated herein.

Important: The following individual(s) is/are authorized to waive discrepancies found in presented documentation, and to be contacted in case of need regarding this transaction.

_____   _____
       (Name, Title, and Telephone #)   (Name, Title and Telephone #)

This Application is made subject to the Letter of Credit Agreement (Reimbursement and Security Agreement) contained herein and executed by us, the provisions of which are hereby made applicable to this Application and the Credit.

PLEASE DATE AND OFFICIALLY SIGN THE LETTER OF CREDIT AGREEMENT INCLUDED HEREIN.

NOTES
(For Bank Use Only)

OMB 3048-0014
Expires 12/31/2006

**Export-Import Bank
of the United States**

**APPLICATION
FOR MEDIUM-TERM
INSURANCE OR GUARANTEE**

This application is to be used for insurance and guarantee transactions with financed amounts of $10 million or less (excluding financed premium) and repayment terms between eighteen months and seven years. Applications for other Ex-Im Bank products can be found on Ex-Im Bank's web site under the "Apply" section.

Additional information on how to apply for Ex-Im Bank Medium-Term Insurance or Guarantees can be found at Ex-Im Bank's web site **http://www.exim.gov/tools/how_to_apply.html**

Send this completed application to Ex-Im Bank, 811 Vermont Avenue, NW, Washington, DC 20571. Ex-Im Bank will also accept e-mailed PDF and faxed applications. Ex-Im Bank will not require the originals of these applications to be mailed. Please note the applications must be PDF scans of original applications and all required application attachments. (Fax number 202.565.3380, e-mail **exim.applications@exim.gov**)

APPLICATION FORM

1. **FINANCING TYPE REQUESTED**

    A. Product   ☐ Insurance
    ☐ Loan Guarantee
    ☐ Finance Lease Guarantee

    B Conversion of a preliminary commitment or a Letter of Interest
    ☐ No   ☐ Yes. The Ex-Im Bank reference number is:

    C. Resubmission   ☐ Check if this is a resubmission of an application that was previously deemed incomplete or was withdrawn for other reasons. The Ex-Im Bank reference number is:

    D. Renewal   ☐ CGF (Credit Guarantee Facility)
    ☐ MTR (Medium-term Repetitive Insurance Policy)

2. **PARTICIPANTS:**

Applicant name:	Duns #:
Contact person:	Phone #:
Position title:	Fax #:
Street address:	E-mail:
City: State/Province:	Nine-digit zip code:
Country:	Taxpayer ID #:
Number of employees:	

    Applicant's role in the transaction: ☐ exporter ☐ buyer/ borrower/lessee ☐ lender/lessor

    Primary contact point for Ex-Im Bank inquiries on this transaction: ☐ exporter ☐ broker (insurance only) ☐ lender/lessor

    This application is for a ☐ supplier credit ☐ buyer credit ☐ finance lease credit

OMB 3048-0014
Expires 12/31/2006

Broker (Insurance Only)

If none, insert "none."   Ex-Im Bank Broker #:

Name of Broker: Phone #:

Contact person: Fax #:   E-Mail:

Exporter: The exporter is the U.S. entity that contracts with the buyer for the sale of the U.S. goods and services. In the case of finance lease, if the lessor is a U.S. entuty and takes title to the goods and services for lease to the foreign lessee, the lessor is the exporter.

☐ Check if the exporter is the applicant. Otherwise, complete the information below for each exporter, including ancillary service providers.

Exporter name:	Duns #:	
Contact person:	Phone #:	
Position title:	Fax #:	
Street address:	E-mail:	
City:	State/Province:	Nine digit zip code:
Taxpayer ID #:		
Number of employees:		

Supplier: The supplier is the U.S. company that manufactures the goods and/or performs the services to be exported.

☐ Check if the supplier is also the exporter. Otherwise, complete the information below for each supplier, including ancillary service providers.

Supplier name:	Duns #:	
Contact person:	Phone #:	
Position title:	Fax #:	
Street address:	E-mail:	
City:	State/Province:	Nine digit zip code:
Taxpayer ID #:		
Number of employees:		

Borrower or Lessee: The borrower is the entity that agrees to repay the loan. The lessee is the entity that agrees to lease the goods and services from the lessor and pay rent under a finance lease.

☐ Check if the borrower/lessee is the applicant. If not, complete the information below.

Borrower's/Lessee's name:	Duns #:
Contact person:	Phone #:
Position title:	Fax #:
Street address:	E-mail:
City:	State/Province:	Postal code:
Taxpayer ID #:	

OMB 3048-0014
Expires 12/31/2006

Guarantor: The guarantor is the person or entity that agrees to repay the credit if the borrower or lessee does not. Refer to the Medium-Term Credit Standards (at **www.exim.gov/pub/pdf/EBD-M-39.pdf**) to determine in what situations personal or corporate guarantors are required for medium-term transactions. Complete the information below for each guarantor if a guarantor is offered or required.

Guarantor name:	Duns #:
Contact person:	Phone #:
Position title:	Fax #:
Street address:	E-mail:
City: State/Province:	Postal code:

Buyer: The buyer is the entity that contracts with the exporter for the purchase of the U.S. goods and services. Check if the buyer is also the ☐ borrower/lessee or ☐ lessor or ☐ guarantor. Otherwise, complete the information below.

Buyer name:	Duns #:
Contact person:	Phone #:
Position title:	Fax #:
Street address:	E-mail:
City: State/Province:	Postal code:
Country:	

End-user: The end-user is the foreign entity that uses the U.S. goods and services. Check if end-user is also the ☐ borrower/lessee or ☐ guarantor or ☐ buyer Otherwise, complete the information below.

End-user name:	Duns #:
Contact person:	Phone #:
Position title:	Fax #:
Street address:	E-mail:
City: State/Province:	Postal code:
Country:	

Lender/Lessor: The lender is the company that extends the Ex-Im Bank guaranteed or insured loan to the Borrower. The Lessor is the company that extends the Ex-Im Bank guaranteed finance lease to the Lessee. Check if the lender/lessor is the ☐ applicant. Otherwise, complete the information below.

Lender's/Lessor's name:	Duns #:	MGA# (Guarantees only)
Contact person:	Phone #:	
Position title:	Fax #:	
Street address:	E-mail:	
City: State/Province:	Nine digit zip code:	
Country:		

OMB 3048-0014
Expires 12/31/2006

3. DETAILS OF COVERAGE REQUESTED

A. Coverage Type ☐ Comprehensive Risk

☐ Political Risk Only [not available for finance lease guarantees]

B. Special Features Requested

Check the boxes for the coverage that apply to the transaction. View the fact sheets describing the coverage on Ex-Im Bank's web site as noted below. Complete and attach the requested forms.

☐ Pre-shipment Cover *Attachment II - Pre-shipment* *Questionnaire required*	☐ Used Equipment *Attachment E required* **www.exim.gov/products/** **policies/used_equip.html**	☐ Co-Financing with Foreign Export Credit Agency *Attachment H required* **www.exim.gov/pub/txt/** **95-10h.doc**
☐ Local Cost Support **www.exim.gov/products/** **policies/local_cost.html**	☐ Foreign Currency Guarantee (specify currency) _____ **www.exim.gov/products/** **guarantee/foreign_curr.html**	☐ Environmental Exports Program **www.exim.gov/products/** **special/environment.html**
☐ Ancillary Service Fees **www.exim.gov/products/** **ebd-m-13.html**	☐ Credit Guarantee Facility **www.exim.gov/products/** **credit_guar.html**	☐ Military/ Security/ Police **www.exim.gov/products/** **policies/military.html**
☐ Nuclear **www.exim.gov/products/** **policies/nuclear/envnucp.html** In addition Nuclear-screening document must be submitted with application.	☐ Finance Lease Guarantee **www.exim.gov/products/** **leaseguar.html**	☐ Lease Insurance **www.exim.gov/products/** **insurance/leasing.html**
☐ Foreign Dealer Insurance Policy *Attachment J required* **www.exim.gov/tools/appforms/** **insurance.html**	☐ Other _____	☐ Other _____

4. TRANSACTION DESCRIPTION

A) Describe Goods and Services. Include make, model, manufacturer/supplier, SIC codes or NAICS (if known) of goods and services, number of units, values and an estimted U.S. and foriegn content. This section does not need to be completed if the exporter attaches a Content Report (www.exim.gov/pub/pdf/ebd-m-58.pdf) or the request is for a Credit Guarantee Facility.

B) Describe the purpose of the transaction. Include answers to the following: Will the goods be used to create or expand production capacity for an exportable product? Are the goods and services destined for an identifiable project? If so, provide information on the total estimated project costs in US dollars. Also provide information as to other sources of financing for the project, including working capital

OMB 3048-0014
Expires 12/31/2006

C) Indicate whether an application for support of this export contract or a related project has been filed with the Agency For International Development, Maritime Administration, Overseas Private Investment Corporation, Trade Development Agency or a multilateral financing agency. If so, include a brief description of the additional support.

5. REQUESTED FINANCING AMOUNTS AND STRUCTURE

Ex-Im Bank support is based on the value of the eligible goods and services in the exporter's supply contract(s) or purchase order(s). The total level of support will be the lesser of: 85% of the value of all eligible goods and services; or 100% of the U.S. content included in all eligible goods and services in the exporter's supply contracts. In addition, Ex-Im Bank may also finance certain local costs, ancillary services as approved, and the exposure fee/premium. Fill out the chart below to determine estimated eligible amounts.

		Definition	US $
A	Supply Contracts or Purchase Orders [If the lessor is a U.S. entity and takes title to the U.S. goods and services for lease to a foreign lessee, the finance lease is the supply contract.]	The aggregate price of all goods and services in all the supply contract(s) or purchase order(s), including local costs, ancillary services, and excluded goods and services. Break out ancillary services in Aii.	Ai Aii
B	Excluded Goods and Services	The aggregate price of all goods and services that are not eligible for or are excluded from Ex-Im Bank support (e.g. goods not shipped from the U.S. and excluded ancillary services). Local costs should not be included in this line.	
C	Total Local Costs	The aggregate price of all goods manufactured in the end-user's country and all services provided by residents of the purchaser's country. Ex-Im Bank may be able to finance these amounts up to 15% of D below.	
D	Net Contract Price	A minus B minus C	
E	Eligible Foreign content	The aggregate cost of any goods produced or manufactured outside the U.S, or services provided by third country personnel or foreign freight costs and foreign insurance included in the net contract price (line D), (e.g. foreign items shipped from the US)	
F	U.S. Content	D minus E	
G	Cash Payment	This amount must be the greater of E or 15% of D	
H	Local Cost Financing Requested	This can be no more than 15% of D	
I	**Financed Amount Requested** (Excluding Exposure Fee)	D minus G plus H	

OMB 3048-0014
Expires 12/31/2006

A. Exposure Fee (Guarantees)/ Premium (Insurance)   Check one box.
- ☐ Ex-Im Bank to finance the fee/premium, which will be paid as the credit is drawn down.
- ☐ Ex-Im Bank to finance the fee/premium, which will be paid up front.
- ☐ Ex-Im Bank will not finance the fee/premium, and it will be paid as the credit is drawn down.
- ☐ Ex-Im Bank will not finance the fee/premium, and it will be paid up front.

B. Transaction Structure.

i. Principal Repayment Term/Finance Lease _____(years). Unless otherwise requested, equal installments of principal will be repaid semi-annually beginning six months after the starting point. In the case of a finance lease, unless otherwise requested, rent will be calculated based on equal installments of principal, paid semi-annually beginning six months after the starting point.

ii Starting Point The starting point is generally the event that marks the fulfillment of the exporter's contractual responsibility. See Ex-Im Bank's fact sheets on starting points and reach-back policies at **www.exim.gov**.
(Check one box.)

☐ Shipment (single shipment)	☐ Services Completion.
☐ Final Shipment (multiple shipments)	☐ Completion of Installation. Specify date:_____
☐ Mean Shipment (multiple shipments)	☐ Project Completion. Specify date:_____
☐ Consolidation Date (Foreign Dealer Insurance Policy only)	

iii Shipment Period Shipments will be completed and/or services will be performed from:
[   ] (month/year) to [   ] (month/year) excluding any acceptance, retention, or warranty period. If shipment is planned for a certain number of days after Ex-Im Bank authorization, so note:

iv. Promissory Notes/Lease Supplements For transactions with multiple shipments indicate:
- ☐ There will be one promissory note per shipment.
- ☐ Disbursements will be consolidated into one promissory note.
- ☐ (Finance lease only:) There will be one lease supplement per shipment.
- ☐ (Finance lease only:) Lease deliveries will be consolidated under one lease supplement.

v. Interest rate
The interest rate to be charged on the guaranteed/insured loan or used to calculate the rent under a finance lease is:

6. REASON FOR REQUESTING EX-IM BANK SUPPORT.

Ex-Im Bank will finance the export of U.S. goods and services if it can be demonstrated that Ex-Im Bank support is necessary for the transaction to proceed. Check one of the boxes below describing why support is necessary.

☐ The exporter is aware that foreign companies are competing, or are expected to compete for the sale. Provide company name, country, and (if known/applicable) the supporting export credit agency.

☐ The exporter is aware that foreign companies manufacture comparable goods and services that are sold in the buyer's market with export credit agency support available. Provide company name, country, and (if known/applicable) the supporting export credit agency.

OMB 3048-0014
Expires 12/31/2006

7. CREDIT INFORMATION

☐ The information requested in *Attachment I: Credit Information* is attached.

8. OTHER INFORMATION AND CERTIFICATIONS

A. General Information - Provide the following:

☐ Credit Agency report(s) on the exporter(s). If exporter has a credit rating of BBB or better, this is not required.

☐ Annex A to the Master Guarantee Agreement (Guarantees only) at **www.exim.gov/pub/pdf/mt-anx-exec.pdf**

☐ Annex A to the Medium-Term Master Guarantee Agreement - Finance Lease (Finance Lease Guarantees only) at **www.exim.gov/pub/pdf/mtlease-anx-exec.pdf**

☐ Lender's mandate letter (required when applicant is a financial institution).

B. Supply Contracts Between the Exporter and Buyer

☐ Sales contract(s), pro forma invoice(s), or purchase order(s) and finance lease(s) are attached.

☐ This is a request for a repetitive sales insurance policy (MTR or Foreign Dealer Insurance Policy) or a credit guarantee facility (CGF) and no contract is attached.

C. Commitment Fee Agreement (Guarantees Only)

For a guarantee, a commitment fee accrues starting 60 days after the authorization of a final commitment and is payable semi annually in arrears on a schedule determined at the time of authorization. The commitment fee is 1/8 of 1% per annum on the un-disbursed and un-cancelled balance of the guaranteed loan. Choose one of the options below regarding the payment of the commitment fee:

☐ The applicant is the borrower or lessee, and by signing the application, is irrevocably committing to pay the commitment fee.

☐ The applicant is the guaranteed lender or guaranteed lessor, and is (check one):

  ☐ signing the application which irrevocably commits it to pay the fee, or

  ☐ signing the application and enclosing with it an Ex-Im Bank standard form fee letter from the borrower at **www.exim.gov/pub/pdf/mt-anx-exec.pdf**. This letter irrevocably commits the borrower to pay the fee.

  ☐ signing the application and enclosing with it an Ex-Im Bank standard form fee letter from the lessee at **www.exim.gov/pub/pdf/mtlease-anx-exec.pdf**. This letter irrevocably commits the borrower to pay the fee.

☐ The applicant is the exporter, and is signing the application and enclosing with it an Ex-Im Bank standard form fee letter from the:

  ☐ borrower at **www.exim.gov/pub/pdf/mt-anx-exec.pdf**. This letter irrevocably commits the borrower to pay the fee.

  ☐ lessee at **www.exim.gov/pub/pdf/mtlease-anx-exec.pdf**. This letter irrevocably commits the lessee to pay the fee.

  ☐ guaranteed lender at **www.exim.gov/pub/pdf/mt-anx-exec.pdf**. This letter irrevocably commits the guaranteed lender to pay the fee.

  ☐ guaranteed lessor at **www.exim.gov/pub/pdf/mtlease-anx-exec.pdf**. This letter irrevocably commits the guaranteed lessor to pay the fee.

D. Anti-Lobbying Disclosure Form

Please refer to the Anti-Lobbying Declaration/Disclosure forms at **www.exim.gov/pub/pdf/95-10d.pdf** and include a signed copy of the appropriate form(s) with your application.

E. Certifications

The undersigned certifies that the facts stated and the representations made in this application and any attachments to this application are true, to the best of the applicant's knowledge and belief after due diligence, that the applicant has not omitted any material facts. The undersigned certifies that neither it, nor its principals, have with in the past three years been a) debarred, suspended, declared ineligible from participating in, or voluntarily excluded from participation in, a covered transaction,

OMB 3048-0014
Expires 12/31/2006

b) formally proposed for debarment, with a final determination still pending, (c) indicted, convicted or had a civil judgment rendered against it for any of the offenses listed in the Regulations, (d) delinquent on any substantial debts owed to the U.S. Government or its agencies or instrumentalities as of the date of execution of this application; or (e) the undersigned has received a written statement of exception from Ex-Im Bank attached to this certification, permitting participation in this Covered Transaction despite an inability to make certifications a) through d) in this paragraph. We further certify that we have not and will not knowingly enter into any agreements in connection with the Goods and Services with any individual or entity that has been debarred, suspended, declared ineligible from participating in, or voluntarily excluded from participation in a Covered Transaction. All capitalized terms not defined herein shall have the meanings set forth in the Government-wide Non-procurement Suspension and Debarment Regulations - Common Rule (Regulations).

In addition, we further certify that we have not, and will not, engage in any activity in connection with this transaction that is a violation of a) the Foreign Corrupt Practices Act of 1977, 15 U.S.C. 78dd-1, et seq. (which provides for civil and criminal penalties against individuals who directly or indirectly make or facilitate corrupt payments to foreign officials to obtain or keep business), b) the Arms Export Control Act, 22 U.S.C. 2751 et seq., c) the International Emergency Economic Powers Act, 50 U.S.C. 1701 et seq., or d) the Export Administration Act of 1979, 50 U.S.C. 2401 et seq.; nor have we been found by a court of the United States to be in violation of any of these statutes within the preceding 12 months, and to the best of our knowledge, the performance by the parties to this transaction of their respective obligations does not violate any other applicable law.

The applicant certifies that the representations made and the facts stated in this application and its attachments are true, to the best of its knowledge and belief, and it has not misrepresented or omitted any material facts. It further understands that these certifications are subject to the penalties for fraud against the U.S. Government (18 USC 1001, et. seq.).

8. NOTICES

The applicant is hereby notified that information requested by this application is done so under authority of the Export-Import Bank Act of 1945, as amended (12 USC 635 et. seq.); provision of this information is mandatory and failure to provide the requested information may result in Ex-Im Bank being unable to determine eligibility for support. The information provided will be reviewed to determine the participants' ability to perform and pay under the transaction referenced in this application. Ex-Im Bank may not require the information and applicants are not required to provide information requested in this application unless a currently valid OMB control number is displayed on this form (see upper right of each page).

Public Burden Statement: Reporting for this collection of information is estimated to average 1 hour per response, including reviewing instructions, searching data sources, gathering information, completing, and reviewing the application. Send comments regarding the burden estimate, including suggestions for reducing it, to Office of Management and Budget, Paperwork Reduction Project OMB# 3048-0009, Washington, D.C. 20503.

The information provided will be held confidential subject to the Freedom of Information Act (5 USC 552) the Privacy Act of 1974 (5 USC 552a), and the Right to Financial Privacy Act of 1978 (12 USC 3401), except as other wise required by law. Note that the Right to Financial Privacy Act of 1978 provides that Ex-Im Bank may transfer financial records included in an application for a loan or loan guarantee, or concerning a previously approved loan or loan guarantee, to another Government authority as necessary to process, service or foreclose on a loan or loan guarantee, or collect on a defaulted loan or loan guarantee.

Directions: Please check each box to indicate information submitted. For information not applicable to the transaction write N/A in the box. All boxes should either be checked or marked N/A. Parts 1 and 2 indicate information required to process a Medium-term Insurance or Guarantee transaction. Part 3 provides a list of items that are optional. Sending information contained in this section may expedite the processing of your application.

Applicant (company) name:

Name and tittle of authorized officer:

Signature of authorized officer:

Date:

OMB 3048-0014
Expires 12/31/2006

APPLICATION FOR MEDIUM-TERM
INSURANCE OR GUARANTEE

Attachment I: Credit Information Requirements

1. INFORMATION ON THE BORROWER:

☐ If the primary source of repayment for the transaction is a corporate guarantor provide only 1a), 1b) and 1 c) on the borrower;

☐ If current information (within the last six months) as described below is on file at Ex-Im Bank, indicate Guarantee or Policy # _____

☐ If the primary source of repayment is the borrower provide the information noted in 1 a) – 1 g) below (note optional information described in part 3):

a) Company description and ownership.

☐ Provide a concise description of the company origin, legal status, facilities, business activities and primary markets.

☐ Provide the name of each owner of at least 10% of company shares and his/her ownership percent.

b) Related party information

☐ Provide names and a brief description of subsidiaries, parent company, and/or commonly owned companies ("related parties").

☐ Indicate which, if any, of the related parties account for more than 25% of the borrower's sales or purchases during the last fiscal year.

☐ Indicate which, if any, related parties extend loans to the borrower or to whom the borrower extends loans, if loans are material to the borrower. Materiality is defined as 10% of the borrower's total assets.

☐ Provide details of guarantees given on behalf of related parties by the borrower, if loans are material to the borrower.

c) Credit agency report

☐ Provide a credit agency report on the borrower not older than six months from date of application, or

☐ Check if credit agency report is not applicable because the borrower is a financial institution (bank), or a foreign government agency.

d) Creditor Bank or Supplier References

☐ Provide a creditor bank reference prepared within six months of the application date. Report should include bank name, address, and length of relationship, amount, currency, and terms of secured and unsecured credit and repayment experience.

☐ If the borrower does not have any financial institution creditors, provide two supplier references. Supplier references should be dated within six months of the application and include years of credit experience, annual sales, the terms of sale, the amount of the last sale, the recent high credit, the amount currently outstanding, details on any past due amounts, and repayment experience.

e) Financial Statements

There are certain requirements for all financial statements, regardless of the amount of the transaction. These are as follows:

i) ☐ Provide financial statements for the previous three fiscal years, as well as interim statements if the latest fiscal year end statements are dated more than nine months from the date of application. When interim statements are provided, also provide interim statements for the same interim period for the previous year (for comparative purposes).

OMB 3048-0014
Expires 12/31/2006

ii) ☐ A summary of significant accounting principles must accompany all financial statements. These should outline, at a minimum, the depreciation methods and rates, valuation methods for inventory, fixed assets and investments and the inflation accounting method used, if any. For construction companies, a description of the revenue recognition method should be included. Additionally, financial statements should break out depreciation expense, gross interest expense, tax expense and current maturities of long-term financial institution or supplier debt, if any.

iii) ☐ For all financial statements that present combined or consolidated results, provide the percentage of total assets, total liabilities, tangible net worth, sales, and net income represented by each entity that is participating in the transaction as the buyer, borrower, guarantor or end-user. A combining/consolidating worksheet would have all this information.

There are certain additional financial statement information requirements that depend on the amount of the financing request as follows:

iv) ☐ For financed amounts of up to and including $1 million: Audited financial statements are preferred but not required for non-financial institutions. Audited statements are required for financial institutions. While English language statements are preferred, Ex-Im Bank will accept Spanish language financials statements.

v) ☐ For financed amounts of greater than $1 million up to and including $5 million: While English language statements are preferred, Ex-Im Bank will accept Spanish language financial statements. Financial statements must be audited by an external independent auditor.

vi) ☐ For financed amounts of greater than $ 5 million: Financial statements must be audited by an external independent auditor. Statements must be in English.

f) Market indications, if available, are as follows:
Name of rating agency: _____ Rating: _____ Date: _____

Include the debt rating reports issued by the rating agency, and if applicable, the prospectus for a debt or equity offering during the two years prior to the application date.

g) Supplemental Credit Questions.
☐ Provide the answers to the questions listed in Attachment C to the Medium-Term Credit Standards for transactions of greater than U.S. $5 million up to and including $10 million where the primary source of repayment is a non-financial institution that does not have market indications. These questions are located on Ex-Im Bank's web site at **www.exim.gov/tools/medium-termcreditstandards**.

2. INFORMATION ON THE CORPORATE GUARANTOR (S):

☐ Not applicable. Refer to the Medium-Term Credit Standards at (**www.exim.gov/tools/medium-termcreditstandards.doc**) to determine in what situations corporate guarantors are required for medium term transactions.
☐ If the corporate guarantor is not the primary source of repayment, provide 1 a), and 1 b) and 1 c) as described above.
If the corporate guarantor is the primary source of repayment, provide the information noted in 1 a) – 1 g)

3. OPTIONAL items which the applicant may attach. These may expedite the processing of your application.

☐ Financial spreads on the borrower and/or guarantor designated as the primary source of repayment.
See Ex-Im Bank's website for spreading conventions, which should be used as guidelines.
☐ Calculation of the financial performance criteria of Ex-Im Bank's Medium-Term Credit Standards on the borrower or guarantor designated as the primary source of repayment.
☐ Mitigating factors for any of the performance criteria that are not met.
☐ Supplemental credit questions as detailed in I g) for deals of less than $5 million.
☐ Translations of Spanish language financial statements, if applicable.
☐ Explanations of any adverse information contained in the credit report, references and/or financial statements, including interims.

EIB-03-02
Revised 6/2005

OMB 3048-0014
Expires 12/31/2006

APPLICATION FOR MEDIUM-TERM
INSURANCE OR GUARANTEE
Attachment II: Pre-shipment Questionnaire

Complete this form only if you are requesting pre-shipment insurance coverage for your transaction. Details on pre-shipment coverage can be found at **www.exim.gov/pub/ins/pdf/eib01-04.pdf**.

Details of Coverage Requested:

a) Provide the reason pre-shipment coverage is being requested: _____

b) Indicate the date the contract was executed or the anticipated date of signing: _____

c) Indicate the estimated period between the contract date and the final shipment date of items: _____

d) Provide a schedule of any progress payments made or to be made by the borrower during the pre-shipment period, or indicate none:

OMB 3048-0014
Expires 12/31/2006

USED AND REFURBISHED EQUIPMENT

Equipment that has been previously owned or placed into service is generally eligible for support under Ex-Im Bank's loan, guarantee and insurance programs, provided certain criteria are met. To be eligible for Ex-Im Bank support, used equipment, including equipment that has been refurbished in the U.S., must meet the following eligibility criteria:

1. To be considered U.S. content, the used equipment must be of original U.S. manufacture, AND, if previously exported, must have been in use in the U.S. for at least one year prior to export.

2. The U.S. costs associated with the refurbishment of the equipment are eligible for Ex-Im Bank support, provided they meet Ex-Im Bank's foreign content policy parameters. Ex-Im Bank can support the lesser of 85 percent of the U.S. Contract Price of the item or 100% of the actual U.S. content of the item provided that (a) the item is shipped from the U.S. and (b) the foreign content of the item does not exceed 50 percent of the item's total production cost.

3. If the used equipment is of either original foreign manufacture or original U.S. manufacture, previously exported and has not been in use in the U.S. for at least one year prior to its proposed export, then Ex-Im Bank will treat it as foreign content and the following applies:

   a. If the equipment is to be refurbished, the used equipment procurement cost is considered eligible foreign content provided that this cost is less than 50 percent of the total procurement and refurbishment cost.

   b. If the foreign content of the used equipment exceeds 50 percent of the cost associated with the procurement and refurbishment of the equipment, then only the U.S. refurbishment portion will be considered eligible for Ex-Im Bank support.

4. Previously exported goods that benefited from Ex-Im Bank financing in the past will be considered eligible for Ex-Im Bank support provided that the original financing has been paid in full and that the equipment has been in use in the U.S. at least one year.

5. The repayment term that Ex-Im Bank offers for used and refurbished equipment will be consistent with Ex-Im Bank's international agreements for repayment terms based on contract value. Ex-Im Bank, at its sole discretion, will determine the remaining useful life of such equipment.

   a. If the remaining useful life of the equipment is at least half the useful life of equivalent new equipment, then Ex-Im Bank may support a repayment term equal to that offered new equipment.

   b. If the remaining useful life of the equipment is less than half the useful life of equivalent new equipment, then Ex-Im Bank may support a repayment term equal to the useful life remaining.

   c. If the sale includes more than one item, including a mixture of new and used items, a weighted average of the useful lives of all the items will be calculated by applying the rules of 5(a) and 5(b) above.

6. Foreign Content for used pieces should be determined by contacting the original manufacturer to ascertain the value on a percentage basis of foreign components contained in the equipment during the manufacturing process. This percentage should be applied to the suppliers purchase price to determine the current value of foreign components. This value should then be adjusted to account for the value of any additional foreign components installed during the refurbishment process.

OMB 3048-0014
Expires 12/31/2006

USED EQUIPMENT QUESTIONNAIRE

Applicant: _____
Buyer: _____
Policy number (for insurance program): _____

Complete a separate questionnaire for each item of used equipment.

1. Product information

Name and description of used equipment:

Equipment History

a) year manufactured: _____ b) hour meter reading: _____
c) mileage: _____ d) where is equipment located: _____
e) how long has the equipment been there?: _____

Is the product under warranty? ☐ Yes ☐ No

Term: _____ _____ Description: _ _____
Has the equipment been rebuilt/reconditioned? ☐ Yes ☐ No

By whom? _____ Location: _____ Date: _____
Does this equipment have an independent mechanical certification, evaluation, or assessment? ☐ Yes ☐ No

2. Export/Import History

Was the equipment previously exported? ☐ Yes ☐ No
Did Ex-Im Bank provide support? ☐ Yes ☐ No If yes, details:
Was the equipment imported to the U.S.? ☐ Yes ☐ No

3. Prices and Costs

Contract price: $_____Foreign content included in the contract price: _____
U.S. supplier's purchase price: $_____ Purchase Date: _____
Cost of rebuilding/reconditioning: $_____ Cost of spare parts included: _____
Description of rebuilding and/or spare parts_____

OMB 3048-0014
Expires 12/31/2006

4. Used Aircraft Only.

Have all airworthiness directives been completed? ☐Yes ☐ No
If no, describe the regulation or directive permits required for continued operation of the aircraft:_____
_____
Number of cycle hours remaining on the airframe and engines: _____
Months remaining before next maintenance "C" and "D" checks: _____
Names of each previous owner and lessee with the corresponding acquisition dates: _____

Signature: _____   Date: _____
Name: _____   Title: _____

(For insurance program):

Broker: _____ Administrator (if applicable): _____

If you have questions about this questionnaire, please contact the Business Development Division (Telephone: 202.565.3936 or Fax: 202.565.3931). For questions concerning large aircraft, please contact the Transportation Division (Telephone: 202.565.3550 or Fax: 202.565.3558).

OMB No.: 3048-0003
Expires   September 30, 2005

(SBA Use Only)	U.S. SMALL BUSINESS ADMINISTRATION	(Ex-Im Bank Use Only)
Date Received		Date Received
C.I.D. No.	EXPORT-IMPORT BANK OF THE UNITED STATES	
☐ Intermediary	JOINT APPLICATION FOR WORKING CAPITAL GUARANTEE	

PART A. PRINCIPAL PARTIES

1. Borrower/Exporter   Please circle the appropriate answer: **New to Ex-Im Bank or SBA?**   Yes   No

Company Name	D&B No.	Telephone No.
Name and Title of Contact Person	Federal ID No.	Fax No.
Address	City	State	Zip

Gross Sales $	No. of Full-Time Employees	Primary SIC Code **OR** North American Industrial Classification System No. (NAIC)	Products/Goods/Services to be exported (Description)
	Small Business as stipulated by SBA Guidelines? Yes No	*Minority-Owned? Yes ☐ No ☐ *Women-Owned? Yes ☐ No ☐	

Management (Proprietors, partners, officers, directors and holders of outstanding stock -100% of ownership must be shown).
(Attach separate sheet of paper if necessary.)

Name and Social Security Number	Complete Address	% owned	*Military Service From: To:	*Race **	*Sex

*This information is collected for statistical purposes only. It has no bearing on the credit decision to approve or decline this application.
**Please use one of the following categories: 1) American Indian/Alaska Native; 2) Black/African American; 3) Asian; 4) Native Hawaiian/Pacific Islander ; 5) White; 6) Ethnicity Hispanic; 7) Not Hispanic.

Affiliate(s) (If more than one, please attach list on separate sheet of paper.)

Company Name	D&B No.	Telephone No.
Name and Title of Contact Person	Federal ID No.	Fax No.
Address	City	State	Zip

2. Personal Guarantor(s) (If more than one guarantor, please attach separate sheet of paper.)

Name	SSN	Telephone No.
		Fax No.
Address	City	State	Zip

3. Lender Please circle the appropriate answer: **New to Ex-Im Bank or SBA? Yes   (If yes, submit annual report.)**   No

Name	Federal ID No.	Telephone No.
		Fax No.
Address	City	State	Zip

OMB No.: 3048-0003
Expires   September 30, 2005

PART B. INFORMATION ABOUT THE TRANSACTION

Loan Amount $	Terms and Fees ☐ 6 months ☐ 1 year ☐ Other (Specify)	Type (check one) ☐ Revolving ☐ Transaction(s) Specific
Interest Rate to be Charged Lender Interest Rate _____% Per Annum	Other Fees or Charges (type and amount)	Renewal? ☐ Yes ☐ No
If Interest Rate is to be Variable: Base Rate _____ Adjustment Period _____ (Monthly, Quarterly, Annually, etc.) Spread _____ Base Rate Source _____ (WSJ, LIBOR, etc.)		Conversion of Preliminary Commitment? ☐ Yes If yes, # _____ ☐ No

Were you assisted by an Ex-Im Bank City/State partner or a Small Business Development Center?	Yes ☐	No ☐	If yes, please identify: Name & Address Contact Name _____ Telephone No. _____

Estimated Total Export Sales to be supported by this Loan $ _____

Principal Countries of Export: (Please identify the top 3 countries.)

U.S. Content _____% (Ex-Im Bank applicants only)

Please estimate the number of jobs to be supported by this Loan:	_____ Maintained jobs _____ Additional jobs created		
Are Performance Guarantees or Standby Letters of Credit to be issued under this Loan?	Yes ☐	No ☐	Percentage of Loan to be utilized for performance guarantees _____%

Please answer the following questions with regard to the "export items" to be exported from the U.S.

Military Is the Buyer associated in any way with the military? Are the items to be used by the military, or are they defense articles, or have a military application?	Yes ☐	No ☐	If yes, please attach a description of the buyer or items, as applicable.
Nuclear Are the items to be used in the construction, alteration, operation, or maintenance of nuclear power, enrichment, reprocessing, research, or heavy water production facilities?	Yes ☐	No ☐	If yes, please attach a description of the items. (Ex-Im Bank applicants only)
Environmental Are the products to be used for an environmental project or have perceptible environmental benefits?	Yes ☐	No ☐	If yes, please attach a description of the items and answer the following: Identify the project: _____ Project Location: _____ Project Sector or Industry: _____ If not related to a specific project, the products are to be used to create an environmental benefit in: _____(Please identify Sector)
Are the items on the **U.S. Munitions Control List** (Part 121 of Title 22 of the Code of Federal Regulations), **OR** do they require a validated export license from the Bureau of Export Administration?	Yes ☐	No ☐	If yes, please attach a description of the items. If uncertain whether a validated export license is required, written verification from the appropriate licensing agency may be required before loan approval. (Ex-Im Bank applicants only)

EIB-SBA Form 84-1   Revised 8/2000   Page   2

OMB No.: 3048-0003
Expires   September 30, 2005

PART C. CERTIFICATIONS

1. **Borrower/Exporter Certification**

The Borrower/Exporter certifies that the facts stated and the representations made in this application and any attachments to this application are true, that the Borrower/Exporter has not omitted any material facts, and that the Borrower/Exporter is not delinquent on any amounts due and owing to the U.S. Government or its agencies or instrumentalities as of the date hereof.

The undersigned further certifies that it is not currently, nor has it been within the preceding three years: 1) debarred, suspended or declared ineligible from participating in any Federal program; 2) formally proposed for debarment, with a final determination still pending; 3) voluntarily excluded from participation in a Federal transaction; or 4) indicted, convicted or had a civil judgment rendered against it for any of the offenses listed in the Regulations Governing Debarment and Suspension (Governmentwide Nonprocurement Debarment and Suspension Regulations: Common Rule), 53 Fed. Reg. 19204 (1988).

Any applicant who knowingly makes a false statement or conceals a material fact in order to obtain a loan guarantee from SBA or Ex-Im Bank may be fined up to $10,000 or imprisoned for not more than five years (or both) under 18 USC 1001.

Please circle the appropriate answer. Attach complete information for any "yes" circled.

1.   Are there any pending or threatened liens, tax liens, judgments or material litigation against the:

  Borrower   YES   NO   **Guarantor**   YES   NO

2.   Has the Borrower/Exporter or its owner(s), or the Guarantor ever filed for protection under U.S. bankruptcy laws?
     Has either had an involuntary bankruptcy petition filed against it?

  Borrower   YES   NO   **Guarantor**   YES   NO

3.   Has the Borrower/Exporter or its owner(s) or affiliates, or the Guarantor ever previously requested U.S. Government financing?

  Borrower   YES   NO   **Guarantor**   YES   NO

4.   Is/has the Borrower or Guarantor: (a) presently under indictment, on parole or probation; or (b) ever been charged for any criminal offense; or (c) ever been convicted, placed on pretrial diversion, or placed on any form of probation including adjudication withheld pending probation for any criminal offense other than a minor vehicle violation?

  Borrower   YES   NO   **Guarantor**   YES   NO

5.   Are all owners and guarantors U.S. Citizens?   YES   NO If no, give alien registration number: _____
     (SBA APPLICANTS ONLY)

Name of Borrower/Exporter*	Date	Name of Guarantor*	Date
Signature		Signature	
Name and Title (Print or Type)		Name and Title (Print or Type)	

*Please attach a signed, duplicate original of Part C for each Borrower and each Guarantor

2.   **Lender Certification**

The Lender certifies that the facts stated and the representations made in this application and any attachments to this application are true, to the best of its knowledge and belief after due diligence, that the Lender has not omitted any material facts, and that the Lender is not delinquent on any amounts due and owing to the U.S. Government or its agencies or instrumentalities as of the date of this application. By signing and submitting this application, the Lender certifies that it would not be willing to make this loan without the guarantee of Ex-Im Bank or SBA.

The Lender further certifies to the best of his or her knowledge and belief, that if any funds have been paid or will be paid to any person for influencing or attempting to influence an officer or employee of any agency, a member of Congress, an officer or employee of Congress, or an employee of a member of Congress in connection with this commitment providing for the United States to guarantee a loan, the undersigned shall complete and submit a Standard Form-LLL, "Disclosure Form to Report Lobbying" in accordance with its instructions. Submission of this statement is a prerequisite for making or entering into this transaction imposed by Section 1352, Title 31, US Code. Any person who fails to file the required statement shall be subject to a civil penalty of not less than $10,000 and not more than $100,000 for each such failure. If Standard Form-LLL is necessary, it may be obtained from Ex-Im Bank or SBA.

The undersigned further certifies that it is not currently, nor has it been within the preceding three years: 1) debarred, suspended or declared ineligible from participating in any Federal program; 2) formally proposed for debarment, with a final determination still pending; 3) voluntarily excluded from participation in a Federal transaction; or 4) indicted, convicted or had a civil judgment rendered against it for any of the offenses listed in the Regulations Governing Debarment and Suspension (Governmentwide Nonprocurement Debarment and Suspension Regulations: Common Rule), 53 Fed. Reg. 19204 (1988).

I certify that none of the Lender's employees, officers, directors, or substantial stockholders (more than 10%) have a financial interest in the applicant. Any Lender who knowingly makes a false statement or conceals a material fact in order to obtain a guaranteed loan from SBA or Ex-Im Bank may be fined up to $10,000 or imprisoned for not more than five years (or both) under 18 USC 1001.

Name of Lender	Date
Signature	
Name and Title (Print or Type)	

OMB No.: 3048-0003
Expires   September 30, 2005

Right of Financial Privacy Act of 1978 (12 U.S.C. 3401)
This is notice to you as required by the Right of Financial Privacy Act of 1978, of SBA/Ex-Im Bank's access rights to financial records held by financial institutions that are or have been doing business with you or your business, including any financial institutions participating in a loan or loan guarantee. The law provides that SBA/Ex-Im Bank shall have a right of access to your financial records in connection with its consideration or administration of assistance to you in the form of a Government loan or loan guarantee agreement. SBA/Ex-Im Bank is required to provide a certificate of its compliance with the Act to a financial institution in connection with its first request for access to your financial records, after which no further certification is required for subsequent accesses. The law also provides that SBA/Ex-Im Bank's access rights continue for the term of any approved loan or loan guarantee agreement. No further notice to you of SBA/Ex-Im Bank's access rights is required during the term of any such agreement.

The law also authorizes SBA/Ex-Im Bank to transfer to another Government authority any financial records included in an application for a loan, or concerning an approved loan or loan guarantee, as necessary to process, service or foreclose on a loan or loan guarantee or to collect on a defaulted loan or loan guarantee. No other transfer of your financial records to another Government authority will be permitted by SBA/Ex-Im Bank except as required or permitted by law.

Under the Paperwork Reduction Act of 1995 (44 U.S.C. chapter 35) and the Privacy Act of 1974 (5 U.S.C. 552a), the applicant is hereby notified that:

(1) The purpose of the information collected in this application is **to determine the eligibility** of the request.
(2) The information collected will be analyzed to **determine the ability** of the participants to perform the transaction and pay for it.
(3) **Public burden** reporting for this collection of information is estimated to average 2 hours per response, including time for reviewing instructions, searching existing data sources, gathering the data needed, and completing and reviewing the collection of information. Send **comments** regarding the burden estimate or any other aspect of the collection of information, including suggestions for reducing this burden to Office of Management and Budget, Paperwork Reduction Project OMB#3048-0009, Washington, D.C. 20503.
(4) This information is being requested under the authority of the Export-Import Bank Act of 1945 (12 U.S.C. 635-635i-7); disclosure of this information is mandatory; and failure to provide the requested information may result in Ex-Im being unable to determine your eligibility for the transaction being requested.
(5) The information collected will be held **confidential** subject to the Freedom of Information Act in Title 5, United States Code, Section 552, and the Privacy Act of 1974 (5 U.S.C. 552a).
(6) Ex-Im may not require the information requested in this application and applicants are not required to respond unless a currently valid OMB control number is displayed on the form (see upper right of each page).

OMB No.: 3048-0003
Expires   September 30, 2005

APPLICATION INSTRUCTIONS

PART A. PRINCIPAL PARTIES

1. **Borrower/Exporter.** Complete this section with information on the individual or corporate borrower. Provide the preliminary SIC code **OR** North American Industrial Classification System No. (NAIC) of the borrower, rather than the product being exported. **Management.** Complete this section for each proprietor, partner, officer or director owning 20% or more of the company.

2. **Personal Guarantor(s).** The personal guarantee of the owner(s) is required in most cases.

3. **Lender.** Leave blank if you are applying for a Preliminary Commitment and a prospective lender has not been identified.

PART B. INFORMATION ABOUT THE TRANSACTION
Provide the loan amount, term and type of loan requested, and answer all questions in Part B. (See also Checklist item 2 below.)

PART C. CERTIFICATIONS
This section must be signed by an authorized representative of the borrower and, if a request for a final commitment, an authorized representative of the lender.

CHECKLIST OF INFORMATION TO BE ATTACHED
(**Note: All Attachments must be signed and dated by all person(s) signing this form.**)

	Yes	N/A
BACKGROUND		
1. Brief resume of principals and key employees, History of business; copy of business plan, if available; identify whether sole proprietorship, general partnership, limited liability company (LLC), corporation and/or subchapter-S corporation.		
2. Explanation of use of proceeds and benefits of the loan guarantee, including details of the underlying transaction(s) for which the loan is needed, including country(s) where the buyers are located.		
TRANSACTION		
3. Attach product literature. If applicable, attach description of items if they are nuclear, military, environmental, on the U.S. Munitions Control List, or require an export license.		
4. Copy of letter of credit and/or copy of buyer's order/contract, if available.		
5. Export credit insurance-related material (policy, application, buyer credit limit), if applicable.		
6. Copy of export license, if required.		
FINANCIAL INFORMATION		
7. Business financial statements (Balance Sheet, Income Statement, statement of Cash Flows) for the last three (3) years, if applicable, supported by the most recent Federal income tax return for the business. SBA applicants must submit the last three (3) years of signed, Federal income tax returns for the business.		
8. Current financial statement (interim) dated within ninety (90) days of the date of application filing.		
9. Aging of accounts receivable and accounts payable.		
10. Schedule of all principal officer/owner's compensation for the past three (3) years and current year to date [if none, please indicate].		
11. Signed joint personal financial statements(s) of each major shareholder(s)/partner(s), owner(s), of the company (with 20% or greater ownership, including assets and liabilities of both spouses) and their most recent Federal income tax return; (not required for venture capital partners).		
12. Estimate of monthly cash flow for the term of the loan, highlighting the proposed export transaction.		
13. Description of type and value of proposed collateral to support the loan (company assets/export product, i.e., inventory, accounts receivable, other).		
14. If Lender, attach Credit memorandum. For SBA Applications, attach D&B Report and Personal Credit Reports on Principals and Guarantors.		
15. For **Ex-Im Bank Applications** only: Nonrefundable $500 application fee for a Preliminary Commitment or nonrefundable $100 application fee for a Final Commitment, whichever is applicable, by check or money order made out to the Ex-Im Bank.		
16. SBA Form 1261 (**SBA Applicants only**)		
17. Copy of IRS Form 4506 (original to be submitted to IRS by the Lender). (**SBA Applicants only**)		

OMB No.: 3048-0003
Expires   September 30, 2005

MAILING/FORWARDING INSTRUCTIONS

Please circle the appropriate answer.

1.   If submitted by a Borrower/Exporter

     a.   Is Borrower/Exporter's requested loan amount in Part B,   YES   NO
        $1,111,111 or less?

     b.   Is Borrower/Exporter a small business, as defined by   YES   NO
        Title 13 CFR Part 121.601?

     If answer to *both* of the above is YES, send entire set of materials to the
     SBA Representative in the U.S. Export Assistance Center nearest you.
     Call (800) 827-5722 for the address.

     If answer to *both* of the above is NO, send entire set of materials to:

     Export-Import Bank of the U.S.
     Office of Credit Applications and Processing
     811 Vermont Avenue, NW
     Washington, DC 20571

2.   If submitted by a Lender.

     a.   **SBA Participating Lenders** must submit with this application a Lender's check
        equal to 0.25% of the guaranteed amount of the loan application with a maturity
        of twelve (12) months or less.

     b.   Is Lender using its **Ex-Im Bank Delegated Authority**?   YES   NO
        If YES, send the application, the Loan Authorization Notice (two (2) originals), the
        appropriate facility fee, and the $100 application fee to the Ex-Im Bank address *above,*
        irrespective of the guarantee amount.

Public Burden Statements

Public burden reporting for this collection of information is estimated to average 2 hours per response, including time required for searching existing data sources, gathering the necessary data, providing the information required, and reviewing the final collection. Send comments on the accuracy of this estimate of the burden and recommendations for reducing it to: The Office of Management and Budget, Paperwork Reduction Project (3048-0003), Washington, DC 20503.

FOR SBA USE ONLY

Loan Officer's Recommendations	☐ Approve	☐ Decline	State Reason(s)	
Signature	Title			Date
Other Recommendation if required	☐ Approve	☐ Decline	State Reason(s)	
Signature	Title			Date

THIS BLOCK TO BE COMPLETED BY SBA OFFICIAL TAKING FINAL ACTION

☐ Approve	☐ Decline	State Reason(s)	
Signature	Title		Date

GLOSSARY

Buyer-Importer-Consignee-Account Party
Party who orders a good or service from the seller in return for payment.
The buyer in the international marketplace.
The recipient of goods or services shipped by the exporter.

Carrier
A *carrier* is any person or entity that transports goods for payment via any mode of transportation.

Custom House Broker
Custom house brokers are persons or entities that are licensed by the U.S. customs agencies to clear merchandise through customs for importers. They also provide services for importers by preparing commercial documents for customs, establishing import licenses, assisting freight forwarders with shipping merchandise through customs, and advising importers on customs regulations. These services are provided for a fee. Many custom house brokers are also full service freight forwarders and vice versa.

Export Management Company (EMC)
An *export management company (EMC)* is an association of manufacturers or a market sector organized to coordinate and develop export markets. Export management companies assist manufacturers with planning exporting strategies and developing overseas markets, establishing relations with overseas distributors, and, in some cases, acting as a distributor for exports.

Export Trading Companies (ETCs)
Export trading companies (ETCs) operate under similar principles as EMCs. Formed along the lines of Sogo Shosha, Japanese trading houses that provide a variety of services for importers and distributors, few ETCs exist today, owing to difficulties in arranging financing with conservative banking policies.

Financial Institutions Involved in International Trade Transactions:
Domestic and international banks
Central banks—government-sponsored financial institutions that regulate currency transactions and other financial transactions.
Government agencies providing assistance for exporting.
International organizations that regulate trade transactions and provide financial and technical assistance for exporters.

Foreign Exchange
Foreign exchange is the transfer of one currency for another based upon market or established rates of exchange.

When dealing with many countries and currencies, the buyer or seller must change currencies as part of a trade transaction. Frequently, buyers or sellers want payment in their own currency. *Foreign exchange* is the transfer of one currency for another based upon market or established rates of exchange. These rates of exchange depend greatly upon a country's rules of exchange, limiting the amount of "hard" currency purchasable using local currency. In most countries, the central bank or finance ministry controls currency exchange; this can create problems or delays due to bureaucratic regulations or currency shortages. These problems often are due to a country's shortage of convertible hard currency, such as U.S. dollars or German marks, making currency exchanges difficult if the local currency is "soft" or less easily convertible. Currency exchange may also add additional costs to a transaction, owing to delays in converting currencies and unforeseen currency fluctuations. Anticipating the future value of currencies is part of trade transactions.

When exchanging currency, it is important that the parties involved in a transaction understand the currency exchange options available. Some exchange alternatives include:

A forward contract can be arranged with a bank, which will sell many foreign currencies at a planned date in the future based upon predictions of the currency's fluctuation. For shorter time periods, banks offer a *spot* rate for currency exchange, which is the bank's up-to-the-minute estimate of the rate of exchange. Banks usually incorporate any fees or service charges for this service into the spot rate.

Future rates of exchange are similar to forward rates, except that they have a fixed and limited number of maturity dates allowed, usually at the end of each calendar quarter (March, June, September, and December).

Less-common forms of exchange are currency *swaps,* where two parties in a transaction agree to switch currencies between each other at a specific date and rate of exchange.

Banks usually incorporate any fees or service charges for foreign exchange service into the spot, forward, or future contract rates.

Freight Forwarder

Freight forwarders are trading companies that provide many services during the shipment of goods and services. Licensed by the U.S. Federal Marine Commission, freight forwarders act on behalf of the shipper for a variety of transactions by:

Preparing merchandise for shipment;
Advising on the most economical and efficient modes of transport;
Booking merchandise for transit;
Packing and loading merchandise;

Preparing, delivering, recording, and receiving all necessary
commercial documents;

Following up on the shipment of merchandise and documents;

Advising the shipper on government regulations and requirements to
be met regarding letters of credit and other payment procedures.

The majority of freight forwarders deal with both air and sea shipments,
but some work only with one type. All services requested are subject
to fees.

Representatives/Agents

Representatives/Agents are persons or entities that act on behalf of the
seller in a transaction. They may represent the seller in a foreign
country by taking orders and generating new customers to improve
the sales of a good or service. Representatives or agents are not directly
involved in the payment process and are paid a commission for their
services.

Seller-Exporter-Shipper-Beneficiary

The producer, manufacturer, or distributor of a good or service.

The seller in the international marketplace.

The exporter who ships his/her goods or services to a consignee, either
an importer or buyer.

INDEX

A

Acceptances, 131–137
Access to Export Capital Program (AXCAP), 140
Advance, cash in, 18–19
Advising bank, 24
Aggregate credit limit, 103–104
Air waybill, 140
All risk policy, marine cargo, 41
Applicant, letters of credit, 20
Asia Mercantile, 47
Asset allocation, 105
Auskunftei Buergel, 47
Avals, medium-term loans, 84–85
AXCAP, 140

B

BAFT, 140
Banker's Association for Foreign Trade (BAFT), 140
Barter countertrade, 119–121
Beneficiary, letters of credit, 20, 24
Bill of lading to order, 139
Bill of lading, ocean, 139–140
Brokers, customs, 72–73
Bulk factoring, export, 80
Business climate, trade issues, 6
Business International Corp., 68
Buyback countertrade, 119–122
Buyer ratings, 98–99
Buyer risk
    cash in advance, 18–19
    consignment, 72
    credit insurance, 40–68
    credit reports, 44–47
    defining, 15–17
    documentary collections, 35–36, 37–39
    forfaiting, 76
    letters of credit, 20–21, 33–34
    medium-term loans, 83–85
    minimizing, 3–5
    open accounts, 69–71

C

Capacity, country, 104
Cargo insurance, marine, 40–42, 67

About TEXERE

Texere, a progressive and authoritative voice in business publishing, brings to the global business community the expertise and insights of leading thinkers. Our books educate, enlighten, and entertain, and provide an intersection where our authors and our readers share cutting-edge ideas, practices, and innovative solutions. Texere seeks to cultivate, enhance, and disseminate information that illuminates the global business landscape.

www.thomson.com/learning/texere

About the Typeface

This book was set in 10.5/14 pt. Bembo. Bembo was created in 1929 by Stanley Morison, for the Monotype Corporation of England. It is based on type cut in 1495 by Francesco Griffo of Italy. This typeface is known for its legibility, due to well-proportioned letterforms, functional serifs, and lack of peculiarities.

Library of Congress Cataloging-in-Publication Data

Thomas, Richard M., 1947–
   Trade finance handbook / Richard M. Thomas, Alan J. Beard.
      p. cm.
   Includes bibliographical references and index.
   ISBN: 0-324-30521-4
   1. Exports--Finance. 2. Export credit. 3. International trade.
   4. International finance. I. Beard, Alan J. II. Title.
   HG3753.T54 2006
   658.15'99--dc22

                                                    2005027458